WITNESS LEE

Abiding in the Lord to Enjoy His Life

Living Stream Ministry
Anaheim, CA

First Edition, February 2000.

ISBN 0-7363-0834-2

Published by

Living Stream Ministry
2431 W. La Palma Ave., Anaheim, CA 92801 U.S.A.
P. O. Box 2121, Anaheim, CA 92814 U.S.A.

Printed in the United States of America

00 01 02 03 04 05 / 9 8 7 6 5 4 3 2 1

CONTENTS

PREFACE

This book is a translation of messages given by Brother Witness Lee in the Chinese-speaking meetings in Anaheim, California on the Lord's Days from October 9 through November 20, 1983. These messages were not reviewed by the speaker.

CHAPTER ONE

ABIDING IN THE LORD
AND ENJOYING HIS LIFE

Scripture Reading: 1 John 1:1-3; 2:27-28; John 15:4-5

FOUR MYSTERIOUS MATTERS

Let us first consider the main points of the Scripture verses cited in this message. In the first passage, 1 John 1:1-3, are three very precious verses. They are precious because they refer to four mysterious matters, all of which are divine. These four divine, mysterious matters are 1) the Word of life, 2) the life having been manifested, 3) the eternal life being reported to the believers, and 4) the believers having fellowship with the apostles and the apostles' fellowship being the fellowship with the Father and with His Son Jesus Christ. The life here is the divine, eternal life, which is a mystery. Then this eternal life produces another mystery, that is, the mystery of the fellowship of the divine life. Therefore, the mysterious fellowship of the eternal life is the subject of this Epistle of John.

THE WORD OF LIFE

At the very beginning of John's Epistle, he speaks of "the Word of life." This means that when we hear "the Word of life," we obtain eternal life and never die. "The Word of life" refers to the Lord of grace who is God incarnated to be a man called Jesus, whom men could approach and upon whose bosom His disciples even reclined. The four Gospels tell us that of all the times He met with people, there was not even one time when they had a so-called worship service. The Bible never says that this incarnated God displayed His power by sitting in the highest place, telling people to worship Him, but instead it says that every time He met with people, He was informal. We may all have the religious concept that whenever we come into a meeting we should be very quiet. If someone shouts, "Hallelujah," we may think he is out of order. However, the Psalms tell us that we should shout loudly and joyfully to the Lord: "Make a joyful noise to Jehovah, all the earth" (100:1). To make a noise is to speak not in a normal voice but to shout loudly. When we come to the meetings every Lord's Day, we should not keep religious rituals and perform orderly ceremonies. We have to realize that we are coming to the Lord of grace to hear and enjoy the Word of life, so we should not feel restrained and remain quiet; we all should shout praises together.

In 1954 I held a conference in Hong Kong. A Western missionary from the Brethren who was teaching in Japan had contacted the brothers. He was attracted by the brothers and therefore came to the conference. Afterward he said, "I really admire this conference. But there was one thing I did not agree with. In your meetings the prayer after the singing of hymns is too loud and noisy." I said, "Brother, shouting is truly in the Bible. Please look at the record where the children of Israel rebuilt the temple after their return from captivity, when the foundation of the temple was laid. All the people shouted with a great shout and the noise was heard far off." Moreover, the book of Isaiah says, "Cry out and give a ringing shout, / O inhabitant of Zion," and "With a voice of shouting declare" (12:6; 48:20). The New Testament also says that when the Lord Jesus entered Jerusalem for the last time, riding on a donkey, "the crowds who went before Him and those who followed cried out, saying, Hosanna to the Son of David! Blessed is He who comes in the name of the Lord! Hosanna in the highest! And...all the city was stirred" (Matt. 21:9-10). The religious people such as the chief priests, the scribes, and the Pharisees held these things in disdain. They were indignant about what they saw, and said, "Do you hear what these are saying?" (vv. 15-16). The Lord answered and said, "I tell you, If these shall be silent, the stones will cry out" (Luke 19:40). This is the mystery of the Word of life.

ABIDING IN THE LORD
BEING THE SUBJECT OF JOHN'S WRITINGS

The second passage is 1 John 2:27-28. Verse 27a says, "The anointing which you have received from Him abides in you." The word for *abide* here and the word for *abide* in John 15:4 are the same Greek word. The emphasis of these two verses is that we must abide in the Lord by the teaching of the anointing so that when the Lord is manifested we may have boldness and not be put to shame.

The third passage is John 15:4-5. These two verses contain two main points, which are really two sides of one important point: the believers need to abide in the Lord, and the Lord will also abide in the believers. This is our general subject: "Abiding in the Lord to Enjoy His Life," and it is also the subject of John's writings. John wrote the Gospel of John, the Epistles of John, and the book of Revelation. In his Gospel and Epistles, he particularly used the word *abide*. The Chinese Union Version of the Bible is one of the best translations, but regretfully the word *abide* is not properly translated in the Gospel of John, and it is correct in only a few places in 1 John. Due to this kind of carelessness in translation, it is unavoidable that much of the true meaning of this word is lost. For example, in John 15, by rendering "abiding in the Lord" as "always being in the Lord," the translators altered the meaning of the entire verse. We thank the Lord that by His mercy and by our own experience we were gradually enlightened by Him to see that this is not a matter of "always being in" but a matter of actually "abiding in."

We were not the first ones to see the truth concerning abiding in the Lord; there have been many saints who pursued the Lord throughout the ages who all saw this truth and wrote many books about it, the most famous of which is Andrew Murray's *Abide in Christ*. Although many saints throughout the ages have seen the matter of abiding in the Lord, according to what we have read and to our knowledge of the truth in the Bible, we can say that there has not yet been a book written which covers the matter of "abiding in the Lord and enjoying His life." Even the word *enjoy* is seldom used in the spiritual books that have been written throughout the ages.

EATING, DRINKING, AND ENJOYING THE LORD

Some people may say that the New Testament does not use the word *enjoy*. But the Bible does speak of eating and drinking. Anything related to eating and drinking must be a matter of enjoyment. The Lord Himself said, "I am the bread of life; he who comes to Me shall by no means hunger, and he who believes into Me shall by no means ever thirst" (John 6:35). He also said, "If anyone thirsts, let him come to Me and drink. He who believes into Me,...out of his innermost being shall flow rivers of living water" (7:37-38). In addition, the apostle Paul said that the Israelites who followed Moses in the wilderness, "all ate the same spiritual food, and all drank the same spiritual drink" (1 Cor. 10:3-4). Then in the book of Revelation written by John, the Lord Jesus promised, "To him who overcomes, to him I will give to eat of the tree of life" (2:7). He also said, "To him who overcomes, to him I will give of the hidden manna" (v. 17). These verses cover the matters of eating and drinking, which are certainly matters for enjoyment.

The whole Bible ends with a promise concerning eating: "Blessed are those who wash their robes"—that is, those who wash their conduct in the precious blood of the Lord Jesus—"that they may have right to the tree of life" (22:14). The entire Bible also ends with a call concerning drinking: "And the Spirit and the bride say, Come!....And let him who is thirsty come; let him who wills take the water of life freely" (v. 17). Therefore, although the New Testament does not use the word *enjoy*, the fact of enjoyment is there. Likewise, the Bible does not use the expression *the Triune God,* but the fact of the Triune God is there. When we baptize people into the name of the Father and the Son and the Holy Spirit, we immerse them into the Triune God. Likewise, when we eat and drink the Lord, we enjoy Him.

Sorry to say, the natural human mind does not have the concept of eating the Lord as the tree of life and drinking Him as the water of life. Even we ourselves had to pass through many years of experience and needed the Lord's leading before we could have the boldness to speak this kind of truth. Before 1958 we rarely used the terms *enjoying the Lord* and *eating and drinking the Lord*. It was not until the spring of 1958 when we had a series of more than forty conference meetings over a period of a little more than a month that we spoke of eating, drinking, and enjoying the Lord. From that time onward we have been speaking about enjoyment. The more we spoke, the more the Bible was opened to us on this point, until we saw that the entire Bible is about eating the Lord, drinking the Lord, and enjoying the Lord.

Genesis tells us from the outset that after God created man, the first thing He did was not to give man the Ten Commandments or to say to man, "Adam, you must worship Me and not forget your source. In addition, I am a proper God who is righteous, moral, holy, and full of light, so you must also behave accordingly and not disobey." This kind of concept is a product that evolved from human culture; it was not God's revelation to man. After God created man, the first thing He did was to bring man to the tree of life and say to him, "Of every tree of the garden you may eat freely, but of the tree of the knowledge of good and evil, of it you shall not eat; for in the day that you eat of it you shall surely die" (Gen. 2:16-17). Here God made a covenant with man, and this covenant was about the matter of eating. In other words, eating is the most important matter related to man's existence; if man eats the right things, he will live longer, but if he eats the wrong things, he will jeopardize his health and invite death. For this reason, after God finished creating man, He immediately spoke to man about the matter of eating. However, because Eve saw that the fruit of the tree of the knowledge of good and evil was good for food, she was tempted and ate wrongfully. This resulted in the fall of man.

After man fell, God came to save him and again brought in the matter of eating. Exodus shows us that the children of Israel not only received God's redemption through the blood of the lamb, but they were also strengthened to leave Egypt by eating the flesh of the lamb and the unleavened bread. Then after they were delivered, they went into the wilderness and ate manna every day until they entered the land of Canaan. After entering Canaan, there was still the matter of eating. God wanted them to go up to Jerusalem three times a year for the feasts, bringing the best tenth of their produce from the land to eat, drink, and enjoy before God (Deut. 14:22-23). Thus, we see that the entire Bible speaks of the matter of eating, but regrettably most Christians overlook this point.

ABIDING IN THE LORD AND ENJOYING HIS LIFE

Eating is an enjoyment, and abiding is also an enjoyment. The purpose of our speaking about abiding in the Lord at this time is that we may enjoy the Lord's life. There is a hymn in Chinese that says, "Abiding in the Lord, His fatness to enjoy; / Abiding in the Lord, His light will brightly shine." This is wonderful!

Before we speak of the Lord's life, we must mention the Lord's redemption. The Bible reveals that God has an economy in this universe. The Greek word for *economy* is *oikonomia* which means a household administration, so it is also an arrangement. Paul's use of the word implies that God established an economy, that is, a plan, an arrangement, to have a great enterprise. Salvation is God's universal economy applied to us. God's salvation is that He wants to work Himself into us.

God is a God of purpose. According to His eternal purpose, He has a plan; this plan is His economy. In His economy God created the heavens and the earth and then created man in such a way that He could work Himself into man in order to produce an entity of dual nature, human and divine, to express Himself. When this economy reaches us, it becomes our salvation. This is the central revelation of the entire Bible, especially of the New Testament. The center of the entire New Testament is the revelation to us of God's eternal economy.

For the accomplishment of His economy, God especially created a spirit in us that He might dispense Himself, the Triune God, into us to be our life, so that we could be one with Him and become a dual-natured entity, an entity with both

humanity and divinity, for His expression. This concept does
not exist in religion, philosophy, or ethical teachings. In the
history of the human race, whether with Confucius in the
East, the philosophers in the West, or the religionists
throughout the ages, no one has spoken of this. This concept
is found only in the Bible. But even in the Old Testament, this
view is mysteriously hidden in types and prophecies. It is only
in the New Testament, especially in the writings of the apostle Paul, that the word *economy* is used emphatically to reveal
to us God's plan and purpose.

A CONTRAST BETWEEN RELIGION
AND GOD'S SALVATION

The natural human concepts, especially those of the
Chinese who have been steeped in and influenced by the ethical and moral teachings of Confucius and Mencius, are full of
the idea of human ethics. The so-called human ethics are
those principles that distinguish us from beasts, principles
that are normal and natural according to human nature.

In addition, people have been influenced by society and
philosophy in general. Thus, there is not a trace of the concept
of God's economy in our minds. Even when we believe in the
Lord, we may think that we have joined a religion. When I
was in elementary school, I had a class on religion which
taught that "religion regulates man's heart." A deeper saying
is that "religion teaches according to its beliefs." This kind of
concept is within us, even if we do not speak it.

Many of us were not clear when we believed in the Lord,
and we did not know what we were doing when we believed.
But as to another matter we were clear: We knew we were
miserable sinners without the Lord and without rest, and as
soon as we believed and prayed, we immediately had joy and
peace; our burden of sin was rolled away, and our misery
disappeared. We thank the Lord for this. But after believing
in the Lord, even though we may not have said it aloud,
within us we had the concept that we were believing in a religion, and in our living we practiced a religion, which means
that we practiced "regulating our heart." For example, before
we believed in the Lord, even though we may not have

committed great crimes, we still liked to take the easy way out or take advantage of others; then after believing in the Lord, we felt in our heart that we had believed in a religion, so we should not do anything bad. This is to practice "regulating our heart." When some children get baptized, their parents tell them, "You used to speak evilly to people, but now that you are baptized, you cannot do that anymore." This is to control the hearts of your children. Sometimes we rebuke the brothers and sisters, saying, "You have been going regularly to the meetings; how could you still do such a thing?" This is religion which regulates the human heart; it is not God's salvation.

The Lord's salvation is not a matter of practicing a religion for the regulating of our heart. In our natural man, it is very easy for us to have a religious concept. The Bible says that wives should submit to their husbands and that husbands should love their wives. It is very easy for us to make such words religious practices for controlling our heart. However, this is absolutely not God's salvation. God's salvation is to dispense Himself into us as our life to become our salvation. For example, wherever I go, a number of people say that my ties are too plain. I reply, "I wear these not because I am under a religious restriction but because I abide in the Lord and He regulates me by His life." Any practice that comes from human teaching or guidance belongs to religion, while any action that arises from the inner sense of life is an issue of God's salvation.

THE MANIFESTATION OF THE ETERNAL LIFE

The Lord's salvation is that He dispenses Himself into us as our life. This is through the mysterious Word of life. First John says that this life which is the eternal life and which has been manifested today is Jesus Christ Himself. The eternal life is mysterious, abstract, and invisible and cannot be felt or touched by anyone, yet this life has been manifested, shown to, and seen by men. The word for *seen* indicates that something is not only looked at but also observed distinctly and investigated clearly in a thorough manner; it compares with the examination by a doctor to diagnose a patient's condition.

John says that the Lord Jesus, who is the Word of life and the inner life, was manifested, and John saw Him and even touched Him with his own hands. Both John and his brother James were ranked with the twelve disciples of the Lord Jesus, and their mother was Mary's sister, so they were the Lord's cousins in the flesh. For three and a half years they were with the Lord Jesus. They not only saw the Lord Jesus but also observed and touched Him. *Touched* indicates that this life was real and substantial to the apostles.

THE CONVEYING OF THE ETERNAL LIFE

When the Lord Jesus was on earth, He said, "I am the bread of life," "I have come that they may have life," and "I am...the life" (John 6:35; 10:10; 14:6). John said that the Lord Jesus is this life and that he saw, handled, and was made sure of Him; then John reported this eternal life to us. He did not report merely by speaking and preaching about it, but he conveyed and transmitted it into us. It is just as the electricity in the electric plant; by our turning on the switch the electricity is conveyed into the lightbulbs to make them shine. The Lord Jesus is God incarnated to be a man of flesh and blood so that men could see and touch Him. We thank the Lord that He did not stay in the flesh; He went through the processes of death and resurrection to become the life-giving Spirit (1 Cor. 15:45) in order to transmit Himself into us. Every time we meet, we receive the transmission of this Spirit into us. This Spirit is the Lord Jesus and the eternal life.

THE FELLOWSHIP OF THE ETERNAL LIFE

The conveying of the Word of life brings in a fellowship, a flow. This may be compared to lightbulbs; if there is no electricity in them, they are not related to one another or in fellowship with the electric plant. But once the electricity is transmitted into the lightbulbs, the flow of electricity brings the lightbulbs into one electric current, which makes them shine and causes them to have fellowship with the electric plant. In other words, the flow of electricity causes the lightbulbs to have fellowship with one another and with the electric plant. Then, if the lightbulbs want to maintain their fellowship, they must abide in the electricity and not cut off the switch. When the lightbulbs abide in the electricity, they enjoy the electricity, and the electricity constantly transmits and supplies the lightbulbs, making them shine and function. If a lightbulb burns out, it cannot function properly because it is not abiding in the electricity; it should only be thrown into the garbage can. This is what the Lord Jesus said: "He who abides in Me and I in him, he bears much fruit;...If one does not abide in Me, he is cast out as a branch and is dried up; and they gather them and cast them into the fire, and they are burned" (John 15:5-6). When we abide in the Lord, we enjoy the Lord as our life. If the lightbulb abides in the electricity, it will shine by enjoying the source of power, and the owner will not throw it away. In the same way, if we want to shine and function, we must abide in the Lord and enjoy Him as our supply and source.

GOD'S SALVATION BEING FOR US
TO ABIDE IN THE LORD AND ENJOY HIS LIFE

God's goal in creating us was not for ethics or morality but for our containing Him. God desires to enter into us to be our life so that we can enjoy this life. How do we enjoy this life? It is by abiding in the Lord. Today the Lord as the Spirit (2 Cor. 3:17) abides in our spirit. Therefore, we need to abide in the Lord. This is not an outward matter of having a religion to regulate the human heart but an inward law of life. Whenever we are wrong, the inward life gives us a sense to remind us we are wrong. In this way we who abide in the Lord do not live a life of ethics and morality but instead live a life that is the Lord's. Our living must be the expression of the Lord Himself. It is not that we are humble because the Bible teaches us to be humble; instead, we are humble because when we abide in the Lord and enjoy His life, we live Him out and He Himself becomes our humility, ethics, and morality of a higher standard. This kind of ethics and morality is of life and is the flowing out of life. It is not of religion, and it is not produced from ethical regulations.

Hymn #476 in our Chinese hymnal says, "Live in the light of life, fellowship with the Lord; / Gaze at the Lord's dear face, follow the Spirit's move; / Pathway of glory take, praising Him day by day; / Live in the light of life." I hope that we can all experience abiding in the Lord and enjoying His life in this way until our living is transformed and we are blessed by the Lord's grace.

CHAPTER TWO

LIVING BY THE LORD IN SPIRIT

Scripture Reading: John 14:19-20; 6:57; Gal. 2:20; Phil. 1:21a; Rom. 8:4

ABIDING IN THE LORD BEING
A CRUCIAL TRUTH IN THE NEW TESTAMENT

In the preceding chapter we said that to abide in the Lord is to enjoy the Lord's life. I remember that not long after I was saved, I was helped to know that the Lord was in me and I was in the Lord. Although I knew this, I was very puzzled by it. Like today's young people, I did not want to be one who just says what others say and follows mindlessly; I wanted to understand clearly. Therefore, I sought to understand what it is for me to be in the Lord and for the Lord to be in me. At the time, however, I did not know how to seek, and I felt that this would be very difficult because to me the Lord was vague, incomprehensible, and abstract. I lived in a house, and after eating I would have food in my stomach. These matters were easy to understand, but how could I say that I am in the Lord? What was the Lord really like? How could I be in Him? In addition, the most mysterious part was how could He be in me? I truly could not figure these things out.

I pondered over these kinds of questions, and I also prayed to the Lord. However, the more I pondered and prayed, the more I was confused. I also studied the Bible, but I felt that it was hard to understand; the Bible gives us only facts without any explanations. It tells us only that we are in the Lord and the Lord is in us, but it does not give any explanations. I spent much time and effort in this study. Gradually, however, I began to understand a little. The New Testament uses the word *in* many times. This little word is insignificant in Chinese, but the mysteries and the main truths in the New Testament all hinge on it. This word is *en* in Greek, and it is used mainly to speak of our being in the Lord.

THE FOUR STEPS OF "ABIDING IN THE LORD" ACCORDING TO THE TRUTH

Actually, in the Chinese language we do not use the expression *in*.... For example, we say that we should walk by love; if we were to say "walk in love," it would sound to us like a foreign language formed with Chinese words. This kind of expression does not sound Chinese at all. Strictly speaking, the Greek does not have words for *by* or *depend upon;* it has only *en* (*in*), and *dia* (*through*). Furthermore, the Chinese words for *in* and *through* are mostly used as verbs, but in Greek the words *en* and *dia* are always used as prepositions, having the same meaning as the English words *in* and *through.*

When the Western missionaries were translating the Chinese Union Version of the Bible, although they were bold to coin a few new expressions, they were not bold enough to properly translate *in...* in many places. For example, Philippians 4:13 says, "I...in Him who empowers me." Because this sounds too much like a foreign language, the Chinese Union Version translated it, "I...by Him who empowers me," again using the word *by.* This sounds Chinese, but the meaning is wrong.

The more I studied this truth, the clearer I became. However, I also felt that this matter became more complicated. Later I made another discovery, that the New Testament not only mentions the word *in* but also uses the word *abide.* John 15 says that we should "abide" in the Lord, but the Chinese Version says that we should "always be" in the Lord. This disregards the main verb. Here it does not mean to be in the Lord always; it means to abide in the Lord. In John 15 the word *abide* is not a light word but a very important one; it means to dwell, not merely to stay awhile. In Greek the words for *home* are *oikos* and *oikia.* When Paul wrote Romans and 1 Corinthians 3:16, the word he used for *dwells* has the noun *oikos* as its principal root, and it was made into the verb form *oikeo* which means "makes home." Then in Ephesians 3:17, Paul strengthens the meaning of this word by adding the preposition *kata* (meaning "deep down"), making it *katoikeo,* which means "deeply make home." This shows us that the matter of abiding mentioned in the Bible is not so simple. There are altogether four steps: the first is "in," then "abiding in," then "making home in," and finally "deeply making home in," that is, making home by sinking in deep roots.

THE EXPERIENCE OF ABIDING IN THE LORD

Although I studied the truth of this matter until I became clear, I still did not understand the factual and experiential aspects. How could we be in Christ? I understood these words in the original Greek, but I still did not know what they meant in reality because I lacked the experience. I could only do my best to read spiritual books, hoping to obtain an answer. In the 1930s I purchased Andrew Murray's book *Abide in Christ,* but after studying it, I still did not get the explanation. Andrew Murray did not present the matter in a thorough manner. At the end of 1941, because of the world situation, I had an opportunity to buy many Greek dictionaries and spiritual books to study. However, after reading them, I still did not get the answer.

Later I went to Taiwan, and I continued to pay much attention to this subject, but because I lacked the experience, I was not able to speak on this aspect of the truth. From 1935 until today, nearly fifty years, I can say that I have thoroughly studied the commentaries and language of the Bible concerning this matter of "abiding in the Lord," but I was unable to find a book that clearly and deeply explained this truth. In the beginning the best book I could find concerning this experience was the biography of Hudson Taylor. From what this book describes about his experiences of John 15, we can say that up to that time he had the deepest experience of anyone in the history of Christianity. Regretfully, though, the language in this book is not clear enough, so I myself could not find the way in. Thus, for the whole of thirty-five years I always felt that I had a lack whenever this matter was mentioned.

Finally when I came to America, I touched on this basic and central truth in the Bible yet again, and because I had more experience, I was able to understand it a bit more clearly. Now, nearly twenty more years have passed, and I can say with assurance that it is easy to speak on this matter because I feel that I completely understand it. For example, in the past I did not know that to abide in the Lord is to enjoy the Lord's life, nor did I know that the real enjoyment of the Lord is to abide in Him. Now, not only do I know this, but I also can speak about it clearly.

For example, when electric wires are connected with the electric power, the lightbulbs and the electrical appliances all "abide" in the electricity. To say "abide" may not be so clear, but if we change the word to "enjoy" or "apply," then it becomes clearer. Whenever the electrical appliances "enjoy" or "apply" the electricity, they can operate. When the electrical appliances "enjoy" or "apply" the electricity, they "abide" in the electricity. In the same way, we, the saved believers, have not joined a religion but have been "connected" with the Lord. The Lord is the spiritual electricity, the electricity of life. We are the electrical appliances, and the word of the gospel is the electrical wire. When we hear the gospel and by the Lord's mercy believe and receive the Lord as the electricity, immediately, just like electrical appliances, we are connected with the "electricity," and we are saved. Therefore, to be saved is to be connected with the "electricity" after the wires have been laid and the appliances have been installed. After the electrical connection has been made, we, the appliances, should take another step to "enjoy" and "apply" the electricity. In other words, Christ has already entered into us, so we should take another step, which is to abide in the Lord.

TO ABIDE IN THE LORD BEING TO LIVE BY THE LORD

We have said that to abide in the Lord is to enjoy the Lord. We can take this one step further by saying that to abide in the Lord is to live by the Lord. When we speak of this, there are not many doctrines involved. We can speak only about the practical experience. Here I would like to ask the young people: You have all been saved, the electrical connection has been made, and you all know that today the Lord is in you; you understand all these doctrines, but do you have the experience? The Lord Jesus said, "He who abides in Me and I in him" (John 15:5). How do you practically abide? Here is an example. Every morning as soon as you rise up, when you enter the bathroom, you should first shut the door and for half a minute pray, "O Lord, thank You for giving me a new day. O Lord, give me the grace to wholly live by You today. Even as I wash, I do not want to wash by myself; I want to wash by You." Just pray a simple prayer like this. Then when you turn on the water, you can pray, "O Lord, I live by You, and I wash my face by You."

Some elderly ones have been saved for a longer time, and perhaps they are thinking inwardly, "I am already a person who is successful and famous, and here I have to listen to this preacher teach me how to wash myself." But this is really practical. I have now passed the age that the Chinese call "ancient," that is, seventy years of age. I am almost to the age Moses spoke of when he said, "If because of strength, eighty years" (Psa. 90:10), and I have had a rich experience of human life. However, I am here testifying to you that I am like a little child every day. For example, this morning I woke up before six o'clock. Because I had received an inspiration, I immediately rose up and quickly sat down, praying to the Lord silently, "O Lord, it is a new day, and I still would live by You." It is very difficult to describe my feeling, but it was in such a spirit, such a heart, that I began to write the footnotes to the Gospel of Mark. As I wrote, I looked to the Lord, saying, "O Lord, I am not writing by myself, I am writing by You." This is the way I practice living by the Lord.

Suppose my wife saw me writing there and said, "A little over a month ago you were so tired that you could not speak. This morning why can't you stay in bed and rest until 7:00?" How should I react? I could get angry and answer, "What? What are you trying to do?" Or I could follow Confucius's moral theories and try to hold my temper and keep quiet, saying in my heart, "Forget it, you are always like this." Or I could neither react nor be annoyed; rather, I could be tolerant, considering myself to be a strong hero, a manly person who should not act like a woman, so I should forgive her and let her go. However, we Christians have the Lord in us, so our reaction should neither be to get angry, nor to behave in a cultured manner, nor to be tolerant. Our reaction should be that "the Lord abides in me." Not only is the Lord abiding in me, but I also live by Him. When I come to my desk, I do not write footnotes first; instead, I first pray to the Lord, saying, "Lord Jesus, thank You for a new day; I want to live by You." Then when my wife comes, it is not I but Christ who lives in me. No matter what she says, I do not get angry, nor do I live according to culture or forbearance. This is because it is no longer I who live, but it is the Lord who lives. In this way I live by the Lord.

When I live by the Lord in this way, the result is that I abide in the Lord. If I do not live by the Lord in this way, even though I am a saved person, I am neither in the Lord nor abiding in the Lord, but I am totally in myself. In the end I will react by being polite, by getting angry, by being tolerant, or by arguing until I am red in the face. Whether I am polite or angry, whether I am tolerant or quarrelsome, I am still in myself. If we are in the Lord, then we will not have these kinds of reactions. We are in the Lord, and the Lord is in us, so we can live by Him.

A PROPER CHRISTIAN LIVING BEING A LIFE IN WHICH WE LIVE BY THE LIVING PERSON WITHIN US

For this reason, the Lord Jesus in John 14 told His disciples, "I will ask the Father, and He will give you another Comforter, that He may be with you forever, even the Spirit of reality;...He abides with you and shall be in you" (vv. 16-17). The disciples heard the word but were unable to understand the mystery of this word. Therefore, the Lord Jesus continued by explaining, "Yet a little while and the world beholds Me no longer, but you behold Me; because I live, you also shall live. In that day you will know that...you [are] in Me, and I in you" (vv. 19-20). This means that after a short while the worldly people would not see the Lord any longer because He was going to be crucified, but the disciples would see Him because He was going to be resurrected. After His resurrection He entered into His disciples to live in them. Hence, "in that day," He lived, and they also lived. Furthermore, they knew that they were in the Lord, and the Lord was in them.

The teachings of Confucius and Mencius can touch people in a way that their conscience is activated. Wang Yang-ming, a Chinese philosopher, said that man must develop his instinctive moral sense and innate ability to do good. He said that if man's actions are only a response to outward teachings and ethical regulations but are not from his inner conscience, moral sense, and ability to do good, then those actions are trees without roots and water without a fountain. We see by this that Wang Yang-ming also taught the doctrines related to the inward aspect of man. But such teachings merely develop the potential ability in the God-created man. As Christians, we do not act according to the function of our conscience or according to the influence of any teaching. We have the living Lord Jesus living in us. We who are saved surely have this kind of experience and know that there is One who lives in us. There are some people who are not very clear about this truth; nevertheless, they can vaguely feel that there is another One who lives in them. When they want to do certain things, it seems He always disapproves and prohibits them.

The story of a Christian's inward being is not a matter of being moved in the conscience by some teachings but a matter of having a real Person living in him. Before we were saved, we did not have this kind of experience; we only had the struggle in our conscience between reason and lust. However, after we were saved, even though in the beginning we were not very clear that there is One living in us, gradually we became clearer that we truly have a Person inside of us. Now, if we would live a normal Christian life, we must live by this One who is living in us. When we live by Him, we enjoy Him and spontaneously abide in Him. If we speak and act by Him, then we remain in Him, and that is our abiding in Him.

When the electrical appliances remain in the current of electricity to enjoy the supply of electricity, they abide in the electricity. In the same way, when we live by the Lord and experience Him, we abide in the Lord. If we neglect living by the Lord in our daily life but only try to pursue abiding in the Lord according to its literal meaning, our efforts will be in vain.

TO ABIDE IN THE LORD
BEING TO LIVE BY THE LORD WITHIN US

We cannot understand this truth merely according to the literal, doctrinal meaning of the words; instead, we must understand it from our experience. According to the letter, it is "to abide in the Lord," but according to experience, it is "to live by the Lord within us." We must live by the Lord in both big things and small things. This is not easy. According to my experience, it is easy for us to be in the Lord when we encounter big or difficult things, but when we encounter small things or fine details in our living, we often neglect to abide in the Lord or live by Him. For example, when the elders fellowship about the affairs of the church, they are very watchful, in fear and trembling before the Lord and not daring to speak loosely. However, in their daily living with their spouses and children, they do not first inquire of the Lord. We often have this kind of old ailment, because we pay attention to abiding in the Lord only in big things but not in small things. This is where we fail.

May the Lord have mercy on us to show us that today we are one with the Lord, and we should live together with the Lord. We have already been married to the Lord, so we should live the marriage life with the Lord. If a husband and wife do not argue about big things but always quarrel about little things, their marriage life is not normal. In a genuine marriage life, there should not be any arguments about big matters or even about little things. The husband should be the head in both the big things and the small things, so the wife should live by him. In the same way, we cannot pay attention to abiding in the Lord only in big things but not in little things. Instead, we should ask our Husband about all things, taking Him as our Head, living by Him.

To abide in the Lord is to live by the Lord. Whenever we live by the Lord, we are abiding in Him. Many brothers have testified that they gain much benefit when they enjoy the Lord every morning because this gets them into the Lord, but as soon as they get to the office, they may not be in the Lord anymore. The sisters are also like this; it is so good for them to rise early to pray and fellowship with the Lord and really get into Him, but once they leave the house to go shopping, they may no longer be in Him. Thus, abiding in the Lord should not be just a matter that happens when we have morning watch, pray, or fellowship with the saints; abiding in the Lord should be a living. When the brothers put on their ties and when the sisters comb their hair, they should pray, "O Lord, I do not want to do this by myself; I want to do this by You." In this way, they will experience abiding in the Lord.

TO LIVE BY THE LORD BEING
TO LIVE AND WALK BY THE SPIRIT

Paul said, "I am crucified with Christ" (Gal. 2:20a). To be crucified does not mean to suffer, as most people would say; that is wrong. To be crucified does not mean to suffer, but it means to die and be terminated. Crucifixion does not cause you merely to suffer; instead, it is to terminate you. However, many Christians today do not understand what this means, and they explain that to be crucified is to suffer. Therefore, they say that to suffer all the time is to "bear the cross daily." Husbands, wives, and children consider one another as crosses which they have to bear, and even landlords and tenants consider one another in the same way. In the church life, you consider the elders, the brothers, and the sisters as your crosses; they all appear to be joined together to give you trouble. However, this is not the cross. A person who is truly crucified does not feel troubled, because he has no more feeling. Thus, crucifixion does not make you suffer; it terminates you.

The result of being crucified with Christ is that "it is no longer I who live, but it is Christ who lives in me" (v. 20b). I have been terminated, and now it is Christ who lives in me. Thus, I can say, "To me, to live is Christ" (Phil. 1:21). This experience equals to live and walk according to the Spirit. Where is the Spirit? The Spirit is within us. We do not need to be taught how to experience this; every saved person knows this. Every saved person knows that the Spirit is living within him. This Spirit is the Lord Himself (2 Cor. 3:17) living in the human spirit. Thus, to live by the Lord is to live and walk by the Spirit. Romans 8:4 says, "Do not walk according to the flesh but according to the spirit." In Greek, the word *walk* here means "live and move." It is not only to move and walk but also to live. This means that our living and moving should all be according to this Spirit within us. To walk according to the Spirit is to live by the Lord. When we live by the Lord, we abide in the Lord, and we enjoy the Lord Himself.

When we view it from this angle and understand it from this kind of experience, we can realize more the meaning of "abiding in the Lord." If you reason even just a little with your spouse, then you know that you are not in the Lord because you have not lived by the Lord. This is just like the lightbulb with a switch that is not securely installed. When the switch is turned on, the lightbulb flickers and gets in and out of the electricity. In the same way, if your inward lightbulb does not shine but is flickering, it means that you are not in the Spirit, nor are you abiding in the Spirit; you are a "flickering" Christian who is not firmly in the Lord. If you want to be in the Lord firmly, then your inward switch must be firm, and it must be always switched on. As a result, you will remain in Christ as the "electricity" to enjoy His supply, and you will shine brightly. This is the proper living that we Christians should have.

Thus, to abide in the Lord is to live by the Lord in all things. Even little things, such as combing our hair and washing our face, we should do by the Lord. We who are saved have not received merely another life within; in reality this life is a Person, who is the embodiment of the Triune God and who is the eternal living Lord abiding in us. This is God's salvation. After we receive God's salvation, we should learn to let the Lord live in us, and we should allow Him to be magnified in us. When we live by the Lord who lives in us, we abide in the Lord. Hallelujah for God's salvation!

CHAPTER THREE

UNCEASINGLY PRAYING
AND IN EVERYTHING GIVING THANKS

Scripture Reading: 1 Thes. 5:17-18; Col. 3:16-17; Eph. 5:18b-20

ABIDING IN THE LORD CONTINUOUSLY

In chapter one we said that to abide in the Lord is to enjoy the Lord's life. In chapter two we saw that for us to abide in the Lord and enjoy His life, we need to live and walk by the Spirit. After such a fellowship some brothers and sisters may not understand and still wonder how we can remain in spirit all the time. For example, a lightbulb functions properly when it "enjoys" and "abides" in the electricity. However, if the switch was not securely installed, the lightbulb does not function properly and, therefore, does not shine steadily. If one is a careless Christian, he is indifferent about continuously abiding in the Lord and does not think there is a problem. A seeking Christian, however, would consider, "How can I abide in the Lord continuously?"

As those who pursue the Lord, we should always pray and petition, longing to abide in the Lord continuously and enjoy His life that we may shine and function every day in a normal way. However, our experience is that we flicker every day. The reasons for our flickering are usually not the big things but the small things. Particularly, our family life and our married life cause us to flicker frequently. For example, both a husband and wife may shine normally immediately after their morning revival, but when they come to the dining table, the husband complains that the milk is too hot, while the wife complains that the husband is too hard to be waited on. Immediately both of them begin to flicker. The newly married ones are not the only ones who are in this condition; even those of us who have been married thirty to fifty years are in the same condition. We can sympathize with one another as fellow sufferers of the same ailment.

I have been saved for almost fifty years and have experienced more problems than you; the problems which you experienced I have also experienced. Hence, I know all the problems in your practical living. I also know that to suffer a relapse from an old disease is easy but to cure it completely is difficult. How then can we solve the problems, the flickering, in our daily life? When you repair a flickering lightbulb, you must first repair the switch and then turn it on; after it has been turned on, do not turn it off again. In your home life, however, your spouse and children, needless to say even you yourself, are capable of turning off your spiritual electricity. Sometimes you are doing well from morning until noon by having fellowship with the Lord and abiding in Him. In the afternoon, however, when the children come home from school and jump around the house, right away you cannot stand it, and your spiritual electricity is turned off by their jumping. Then you quickly repent and confess, praying to the Lord for the cleansing of His precious blood. In this way the switch is turned back on. But after another five minutes, your electricity is turned off again. This is our problem.

UNCEASINGLY PRAYING AND
IN EVERYTHING GIVING THANKS ENABLING US
TO ABIDE IN THE LORD CONTINUOUSLY

Hence, the best way to keep the spiritual electricity from being turned off is to install a safety box and lock the switch in. How do you lock it in? The way is to "unceasingly pray and in everything give thanks." This is not doctrinal but experiential. In doctrine, no one can connect "unceasingly pray and in everything give thanks" with "abiding in the Lord." There is one book in the New Testament that specifically covers the matter of abiding in the Lord, and that is the first Epistle of John. Yet in such a book there is no mention at all of unceasingly praying and in everything giving thanks. Knowledge is one thing, while experience is another. Often those with a

Ph.D. are inferior to those who are experienced. Therefore, I am not telling you about knowledge or doctrine; I am speaking about experience. The secret, the key, to remaining in the enjoyment of the Lord is prayer and thanksgiving.

We all can understand what it means to pray and to give thanks. When we pray, we are shining within, but if we also give thanks, we will become enlivened within. Prayer may be likened to connecting the wires, and thanksgiving, to shining the light. Sometimes our "wires" have been connected, yet it seems that we do not sense any reaction. The light does not shine if there is only prayer but no thanksgiving. Therefore, if we want to have a life that is always shining without flickering, we need to pray unceasingly and give thanks in everything. According to our experience, if we pray and also give thanks, even if before we were not abiding in the Lord, we will spontaneously enter into the Lord and abide in Him. If we want to get in and not come out but remain inside all the time, we need to pray unceasingly and give thanks in everything.

A vile sinner needs only to believe and repent, praying to the Lord, "Lord Jesus, I am truly a vile sinner. I pray that You save me." Immediately the "connection" is made, and Christ enters into him. This sinner, however, still has to say, "Lord Jesus, I really thank You." Then the light in him will shine, and he will abide in the Lord. Hence, whether we are believers or sinners, we all need to abide in the Lord through prayer and thanksgiving.

THE CHRISTIAN LIFE ULTIMATELY BEING A MATTER OF GIVING THANKS IN EVERYTHING

Apparently, we cannot find the truth of giving thanks in everything throughout the whole Bible. Actually, the Bible, which is a book of mysteries, contains an untold measure of light beneath the surface. Among the twenty-seven books of the New Testament, only three—1 Thessalonians, Colossians, and Ephesians—mention the matter of giving thanks in everything. All three of these books were written by the apostle Paul, and their contents show a sequence that is mysterious and wonderful.

The first of these books, 1 Thessalonians, speaks of how we can be saved and how we should have a holy life so that our spirit, soul, and body may be wholly sanctified, making us ready to meet the Lord at His coming. This concerns a proper, general Christian life. The second book is Colossians, which concerns Christ and which eventually speaks about experiencing Christ. The life of experiencing Christ is a life of giving thanks in everything. Not only is the proper, general Christian life a life of giving thanks in everything, but also the life of experiencing Christ is ultimately a matter of giving thanks for all things. The third book, Ephesians, which is a sister book to Colossians, concerns the church, and at the end it speaks about the experience of the church. We can have the church life only by living in the spirit. Likewise, such a church life is a matter of giving thanks in all things.

Hence, we can see clearly that whether it is the proper Christian life, the life of experiencing Christ, or the church life, each concludes with giving thanks in all things. Our Christian life is of three stages: the general Christian life; the life of experiencing Christ, abiding in Christ, and living Christ; and the church life, the life of experiencing the Body. Every stage of our Christian life involves the giving of thanks in everything. Our Christian life becomes deformed whenever it is separated from the matter of giving thanks in all things.

The first ten years after I was saved was a life in 1 Thessalonians. As a saved one, I desired to learn to be sanctified in everything and to preserve myself daily from uncleanness that my spirit, soul, and body might be preserved and I could be ready to meet the Lord. This was the initial stage of my Christian life. As I gradually progressed, I began to study the Bible and some of the books concerning the inner life; thus, I gained more knowledge concerning Christ. I began to know Christ as my life. I also began to realize that the life which God wants us to live is not merely a life of holiness that is without uncleanness but a life of being filled with and saturated by Christ. Unless I live a life of being filled with and saturated by Christ, my living is not much different from the living based on the moral teachings of the Chinese philosophers. These philosophers taught people to develop their "bright virtue" and to be blameless and pure, yet they did not have Christ in them. We, however, have Christ in us. Hence, Christ should be our all, and our living must be Christ. This is the second stage of the Christian life.

After experiencing Christ in a deeper way, I began to realize that the life of experiencing Christ is not for me individually but for His church and for the testimony of the church. We have all received Christ by grace, and the result is that we are the church. Hence, eventually we need to live in the church, to have the church life. This is the deepest stage of the Christian life. All these three stages of life conclude with the matter of giving thanks in everything. Without giving thanks in all things, we cannot live the proper Christian life.

PRAYER AND THANKSGIVING
BEING A CHRISTIAN'S SPIRITUAL FEET

Prayer and thanksgiving are like our two feet; one foot cannot walk without the other. Prayer without thanksgiving will not work; thanksgiving without prayer also will not work. Hence, we must not only pray but also give thanks, and we must give thanks with prayer. We must do both simultaneously. It does not matter which comes first. As long as you have both, you can conveniently walk on the pathway of your Christian life. Likewise, when we take care of and nourish the new ones, we should teach them not only to pray but also to give thanks.

As you walk on the spiritual pathway, do not ask whether you should start with your right foot or with your left. Actually, to this day I still do not know which foot goes first when I walk. If you pay your attention to trying to decide which foot should go first, you will probably have difficulty in walking. Therefore, in our Christian life we should pray and give thanks, and we should give thanks and pray; we should always walk this way. Perhaps before you go to bed, you pray first and then give thanks, but in the morning when you get up, you give thanks first and then pray. Prayer and thanksgiving are the Christians' spiritual feet. If one foot is missing, walking becomes extremely difficult; if both feet are missing, walking becomes impossible. If Christians do not pray and give thanks, they cannot have a proper Christian life.

UNCEASINGLY PRAYING

How can we pray unceasingly? When I first became a Christian, I was amazed when I read in the Bible that we should unceasingly pray. I asked myself, "Does this mean that I should devote all my time praying and not do anything else? Then what should I do about eating, washing, going to work, and sleeping?" In the literal sense, this is illogical. If Paul were here, I would ask him, "Brother Paul, you told us to pray without ceasing. How is it possible?" Paul did not say, "Pray constantly" or "pray continually"; instead, he said, "Pray unceasingly." "Pray unceasingly" is a stronger expression than "pray constantly" or "pray continually." Constant or continual conveys only a sense of continuation. For example, I eat three meals a day; this is continual. I release a message every week, that is, I preach once every seven days. This is a continual preaching. However, if I eat or preach unceasingly, this means that I eat or preach all the time, twenty-four hours a day. Therefore, how can we pray without ceasing? Since my youth I tried to solve this problem, yet I could not find the answer.

However, every spiritual matter can be confirmed by practical things. We thank the Lord for this. This is God's sovereign arrangement. For example, Hymn #231 in the Chinese hymnal borrows the good wine and sweet honey of our daily life, the great sea and vast ocean on earth, and the sun and moon in heaven to depict the Lord's love. All these things describe the Lord's love. Furthermore, the third stanza of *Hymns*, #482, says, "This the secret nature hideth, / Harvest grows from buried grain; / A poor tree with better grafted, / Richer, sweeter life doth gain." This is true. Then, what can we find in nature to signify unceasing prayer? Eventually, I found that there is only one thing: our breathing.

There is no way that we can do anything continuously, without interruption. According to God's law, within twenty-four hours there must be a night, and we must have eight hours of sleep. If you go to bed and rise up every day at a regular time, you will have a healthy body. George Müller, who lived to be over ninety years of age, said, "We Christian workers travel frequently, but we must avoid traveling at night because God has ordained nighttime for our sleep. If we work at night instead of sleeping, we act against God's ordination." This is true. By practicing a regular schedule of sleep at night we will not feel tired when we work during the day. But if we were to sleep during the day, we would not sleep well. Also to work until deep into the night would be very tiring, yet to sleep at night is very fitting. This is God's law.

Not only is there a night for rest within each day, but there is also a day for rest every seven days. This is not a Jewish regulation; this is God's ordination. However, today many people ruin such a day of rest and become even more tired by their indulgences. In God's creation almost everything has an intermission, but in God's ordination there is one thing that has no interruption, and that is our breathing. Eating, drinking, and sleeping are intermittent; only breathing is not intermittent. When breathing is interrupted, the result is death. While you are eating, drinking, and sleeping, you must still breathe. Therefore, our uninterrupted breathing is actually a picture of our unceasing prayer.

THE PRACTICE OF UNCEASING PRAYER

It is easy to explain the truth concerning unceasing prayer, but it is very difficult to practice it. We can breathe continuously, but how can we pray unceasingly in the same way we breathe? Yes, I have found out that breathing is a secret in nature which is very logical, because it is the only thing among the great things of human life that is unceasing. However, I could not understand how we can pray unceasingly as we do in breathing. We cannot use our physical organs incessantly; if we do, we will have problems. For example, after talking too much, our throat is tired and needs a rest. When our hands become too tired after carrying a heavy load for a long time, they need a rest. But among the organs of our body created by God, there is one that is used continuously, and that is our nose, which we use for breathing. We have never

heard anyone say that he has been using his nose for breathing all the time and, therefore, his nose is tired and needs a
rest. All our organs get tired, but we thank and praise the
Lord that our breathing organ never gets tired.

Therefore, what does it mean to "unceasingly pray"? We
must understand and realize that we have a spirit within us,
which is our spiritual breathing organ. The reason we do not
want to pray or cannot pray is that we basically do not use our
spirit. To pray, we must use our spirit. Whenever we use
our spirit, we are enlivened. The first function of our spirit is
to pray. Your spirit prays automatically even without your
prompting. Hence, in order to pray unceasingly, you must not
interrupt your spirit's activity. Instead, you must allow your
spirit to be active all the time.

The spirit's activity is to pray to the Lord. Even without
opening my mouth to make a sound, my spirit automatically
"breathes" in me to have fellowship with the Lord. Sometimes
I may feel deflated; at that time I need to take a deep breath
and call, "O Lord Jesus!" I may not make a sound, but still I
am breathing in the Lord. We all should practice this kind of
inaudible yet uninterrupted prayer.

When I was newly saved, I felt that it was very hard to
pray unceasingly. Sometimes I stopped what I was doing in
order to pray. Others thought it was strange and wondered
why I would stop in the middle of my task and go away to
pray. At that time I did not know what it meant to exercise my
spirit; I never even heard of such an expression. It was not
until later that I realized that there is no need for us to put
aside the task at hand in order to devote ourselves to pray. To
pray unceasingly means that we should always exercise our
spirit to contact the Lord.

We are fallen people from our birth, and the spirit of a
fallen man is dead. We have the organ, but it is dead and has
lost its function; we basically do not use it. Hence, when we
were young, we did not use our spirit. When we went to
school, no one taught us to use our spirit, and we did not use
our spirit in our daily walk. It was not until we heard the
gospel and our conscience was enlightened by the shining of
the light of the gospel that we were touched in our conscience,

which is a part of our spirit. We then began to repent and
confess. When we repented and confessed, that was the exercise of our spirit. It was at that moment that our spirit was
activated, was made alive, and was no longer deadened. In
this way we were saved.

At the time we were saved, our spirit was made alive. However, we still did not become accustomed to exercising this
organ, and even when we prayed, we did not use it very much.
In that period of time we had two kinds of prayer. One kind
was that we closed our eyes and prayed in a routine way to
the heavenly Father for several matters and then asked Him
to give us peace. Another kind was when a great calamity
came upon us. At such a time, even a Christian who does not
know how to pray will be able to cry out, "O Lord Jesus, rescue
me!" When we are so hard pressed, our spirit is stirred even
though we may not know how to use it. This kind of prayer is
a genuine prayer because our spirit truly has been exercised.
All of us need to be reminded that we should not wait until a
calamity comes to call on the Lord. Today we must exercise
our spirit to pray. We should not pray from our mind or only
because of an outward circumstance.

Forty years ago, by the Lord's mercy, I learned to practice
praying by exercising my spirit. Now I can say that I am
accustomed to using my spirit. Just as we walk when our feet
move, so we pray when our spirit moves. Hence, we all need to
exercise our spirit that it may become living and strong. The
secret to our abiding in the Lord and enjoying His life is that
our spirit is living. Just as our eyes are our seeing organ, so
our spirit is our praying organ. The function of our eyes is to
see, and the function of our ears is to hear. Likewise, the function of our spirit is to pray. God created such a spirit for us.
Therefore, we need to practice using our spirit that our spirit
may be living.

Furthermore, we need to practice doing everything in our
spirit and according to our activated spirit. If we do not move
according to our activated spirit, we will practice religion.
When our spirit is active, that is prayer; when our spirit is
inactive, that is religion. Even when eating and drinking we
need to practice having an active spirit. When our spirit is

active, we pray. When we live and walk in our activated spirit, we pray unceasingly, and spontaneously we abide in the Lord and enjoy Him as our life.

CHAPTER FOUR

NOT QUENCHING THE SPIRIT
OR NEGLECTING THE LORD'S WORD

Scripture Reading: 1 Thes. 5:17-21; Col. 3:16-17; Eph. 5:18b-20

Prayer: O Lord, we thank and praise You from the depths of our heart for gathering us once again. Your Spirit dwells in us, and also Your word is in us. We truly offer up our worship to You from the depths of our being because You have drawn us to seek You and Your word. Cleanse us again with Your precious blood. We trust in Your presence and the moving of Your Spirit; we do not trust in what we can do. Lord, we pray that You bless every one of us. We can sow and plant, but we cannot give life to others or cause them to grow. Lord, only You can do these things. For this reason, we really look to You to take care of the needs of everyone, especially the newly saved ones, that we may be full of light within and have Your word as a base to know assuredly that we have been saved, and that every one of us may become living to flow out Your life from within us.

O Lord, give us the utterance and pour out Yourself again upon us so that Your thought, Your feeling, and Your rich word may dwell in us. May what we speak be only Yourself. We pray that You come to every one of us that we may gain You right now.

O Lord, we can never forget Your enemy, Satan, the evil one. We ask You to crush him, even crush him now from within us. We bind him in Your name; we plunder his goods and release those who are bound by him. O Lord, set every one of us free—from sin, from the bondage of the world, and from the oppression of Satan. O Lord, glorify Your own name.

We give You all the honor and glory. In Your own lovely name. Amen.

ABIDING IN THE LORD BEING A MYSTERY THAT CAN BE EXPERIENCED

In the previous chapter we clearly saw that a living way for us to abide in the Lord is to pray unceasingly and to give thanks in all things. The phrase *abiding in the Lord* is truly a mystery to the Chinese, but I believe that from the previous chapters we all must have gained some understanding. Although abiding in the Lord is a mystery, it is not an incomprehensible mystery. Perhaps we do not thoroughly understand it, but we can experience it. Take the human body as an example. A doctor will tell us that after a lifelong study, he still is very limited in his understanding of the human body. The more a doctor becomes a specialist, the more he feels that he understands so little. The longer a doctor practices medicine, the more he feels that his knowledge is short because the human body is too mysterious. In other words, he does not know all there is to know.

Not only so, there is an abstract system in man. Our heart, lungs, skin, bones, and so forth belong to a tangible, physical system; but our heart, mind, emotion, will, conscience, soul, and so forth belong to an intangible, nonphysical, psychological system. This nonphysical part is even harder to understand and explain. I have lived for over eighty years, but today if you ask me how to distinguish emotion, feeling, sentiment, and love, it would be very difficult for me to answer. Love is something of our heart; hence, it is an inward matter. Then, what is emotion or sentiment? How do we distinguish them from love? It is really hard to explain. Furthermore, in the deepest part of our being there is a spirit, which is an inward matter even more mysterious. The Bible tells us that God is Spirit (John 4:24); it also tells us that God not only stretched forth the heavens and laid the foundations of the earth but also formed a spirit within man (Zech. 12:1). From this verse we see that the Bible considers the human spirit as important as the heavens and the earth.

The matter of the spirit within man is truly mysterious and difficult to explain. Although the Bible speaks of the heart, its emphasis is still on the spirit. Regrettably, the Western missionaries who translated the Bible into Chinese were not very clear regarding the heart and the spirit, nor did the Chinese scholars who helped them in the translation clearly understand these terms, even though these scholars had high literary degrees. The result is that they combined these two words and produced a compound term, *heart-spirit*. Hence, this compound word *heart-spirit* occurs frequently in the Chinese Union Version. It is difficult enough to understand the heart and the spirit separately; putting these two mysterious items together makes it almost impossible for us to understand them.

Some of the hymns, following the usage of the Chinese Union Version, also use this compound word. When we were collecting such hymns for our hymnal, we tried to separate the two words by a comma. The heart and the spirit are not one item but two separate items. Despite the fact that they are hard to distinguish, they can be experienced by us. The same is true with the matter of abiding in the Lord. I trust that after considering these few chapters, you will already have had some experiences of abiding in the Lord. Even though you could not explain them, you surely will have had the taste of them.

GIVING THANKS IN ALL THINGS

In addition to abiding in the Lord, we need to give thanks in all things and to pray unceasingly. Here we must first say something about some language problems. Those who read the Bible know that the problems with language come from the tower of Babel. In the Greek text the clause *in everything give thanks* does not have the notion of *blessings* as the Chinese translation indicates. The Chinese translators rendered this clause as *in everything thank the blessings* because, according to its strict sense in Chinese, the word *thank* is a transitive verb and therefore requires a direct object; there would be no justification for not having a direct object. For this reason the word *blessings* was added. But such an addition distorts the meaning of this particular clause. In our experience we should not "thank the blessings"; rather, we should thank the Lord Himself. It is not "thanking the blessings"; it is giving thanks.

To pray unceasingly means to use our spirit, to exercise our spirit. For example, we use our feet to walk and our mouth to eat and talk. Likewise, we use our spirit to pray, and when we pray, we use our spirit.

The many years of my speaking for the Lord in serving Him may be divided into several periods. Before 1943 the emphasis of my messages leaned heavily on the truth. I spoke on many truths, such as God's selection, predestination, sanctification, and justification. Forty-two of the sixty topics in the book entitled *Basic Truths in the Bible* were written by me in 1943; in the previous year I had spoken on these forty-two topics, resulting in a great revival. When the revival came, I began to suffer persecutions. First, the Japanese put me into prison and tortured me for a month before releasing me. Due to this kind of treatment, after I got out of prison, I became ill with tuberculosis, and I rested in bed for half a year according to my doctor's charge. At the time of my release the Japanese would not let me go but still required me to report all my movements subsequent to the release. But then when I became sick with tuberculosis, they relented and let me go. After a year my health improved a bit, and I then escaped to Chingtao to rest there for another year and a half until my health was recovered.

During the period of my recuperation, the Lord shined on me, showing me that although my preaching from 1932 to 1942 resulted in a great revival, there was a great shortage of life in my messages. There was much truth but too little life. At that time the Lord showed me the tree of life and that this line runs through the entire Bible. The Bible begins with the tree of life and also ends with the tree of life. The Bible is altogether concerning life. The Lord Jesus said, "I am...the life" (John 14:6); He also said, "I am the true vine" (15:1). Therefore, we can conclude that He is the tree of life. He came that we might have life and have it more abundantly (10:10). This enlightening and seeing caused me to have a great turn.

In 1946 after my health was restored and I was able to travel for the ministry, I went to Nanking. At that time, due to the flow of the revival in Chefoo, Nanking also had a revival. I arrived in Nanking and began to minister, speaking the word of life. I kept speaking from Chefoo and Chingtao to Nanking, then to Shanghai, and eventually to Taiwan and southeast Asia until 1960. For about twenty years I kept speaking on life. But honestly speaking, although I spoke of life there was not much life, because, I feel, I was not that living. Therefore, I prayed, asking the Lord what the problem was and how it could be that I spoke of life yet I was not living.

A CHRISTIAN NEEDING NOT ONLY TO HAVE THE LORD AS LIFE BUT ALSO TO LIVE IN SPIRIT

Then the Lord showed me that it is not adequate to have life and yet be without the Spirit. From then on I began to speak about the Spirit. At the same time, I also wrote a number of hymns. Under the Lord's leading eighty-five hymns were written within two months. Every morning when I rose up, the first thing I did after I prayed was to write hymns. At that time in my reading of the Bible, the light that came to me was all concerning the Spirit. I came to Numbers 21, which says that when the Israelites were thirsty in their journey, Moses told them to dig the well for water. While they were digging, they sang, "Spring up, O well! Sing to it! / The well, which the leaders sank, / Which the nobles of the people dug, / With the scepter, with their staffs" (vv. 17-18). As a result, they dug out the living water. I received an inspiration from this, seeing that today we also must dig the well. Thus, I wrote Hymns, #250: "Spring up, well, with water; / Dig Thou, Lord, completely; / Dig away all barriers / That Thy stream flow through me."

In this way I spoke exclusively of the Spirit. Deep down in me I saw that Christians in general had made a serious mistake; they did not care one bit for the Spirit. It seems that it does not matter to them whether or not there is the Spirit. They think, "We have already been washed in the precious blood of Jesus, and since He already died for us on the cross, we have been saved through faith in Him. Now we need only to look to Him to take care of us so that we may be good persons, fearing God, reading the Bible, and praying. This is good enough, and there is no need to care for the Spirit." For this reason Christians in general became deadened; this led to the rise of the Pentecostal movement in the middle of the last century.

The birth of the Pentecostal movement was due to the fact that there were some believers who felt that Christians in general were too dry. They felt the need to pray with loud voices and in a particular way, even to pray without food or sleep, praying all day and all night continuously for several days. They believed that by praying in this way Christians could obtain the particular experience of having the Spirit of power from above come upon them suddenly that they might receive the baptism of the Spirit which would enable them to speak in tongues. In this way they would receive the Holy Spirit. When I first believed in the Lord, someone asked me if I had received the Holy Spirit. I felt bad and also perplexed because I was not clear whether or not I had. I asked him how to receive the Holy Spirit, and he said that he did not know either. Actually, both of us had the Holy Spirit but we did not know it then.

When the Pentecostal movement came to Northern China, at first those in the Southern Baptist denomination resisted it because of their theological belief, but eventually they succumbed to it because the tide of the movement was too strong. Therefore, in 1932 in a Southern Baptist congregation, I attended such a Pentecostal meeting for the first time with the desire to receive the Holy Spirit. Eventually, when I saw them shouting and jumping, I simply could not say amen from within. Therefore, I gave it up and set about to do my own research.

GOD PASSING THROUGH VARIOUS PROCESSES
TO BECOME THE LIFE-GIVING SPIRIT

When the Lord led me to sense my need of the Spirit, I applied special effort to carefully pursue this matter, praying and studying the Bible diligently. As a result, I saw that it was clearly revealed in the Bible and also confirmed by my experience. The Bible tells us that on the one hand, it is not enough for us merely to fear God and behave properly as good human beings; and on the other hand, it is also not enough solely to seek for power from on high to be poured upon us so that we may speak in tongues. The Bible reveals that the Triune God has a plan. In the Old Testament He did all the preparation work. Then at the beginning of the New Testament He Himself was born to be a man and lived on earth for thirty-three and a half years. Eventually, He went to the cross and was crucified there in His human body in order to bear our sins and redeem us by shedding His blood for us. He also died for us to terminate the old creation and to accomplish redemption. Then He was buried, and He rested, and on the third day He was resurrected from the dead.

In His resurrection He was transfigured from the flesh into the Spirit. This is what 1 Corinthians 15:45 means: "The last Adam became a life-giving Spirit." As such a Spirit, He is the breath, or *pneuma* in Greek. On the evening of the day of the Lord's resurrection, the disciples assembled in a room with the doors and windows shut for fear of persecution from the Jews. They were sorrowful because they had seen with their own eyes the arrest and crucifixion of the Lord Jesus, who had been with them in His flesh, and they also had seen Him buried in a tomb. They thought now that all was finished. It was at this juncture that the Lord Jesus came into their midst and breathed into them, saying, "Receive the Holy Spirit" (John 20:22). Then He disappeared.

The Bible tells us that afterwards the Lord Jesus was with the disciples for forty days in this manner, training them to know Him as the Spirit. The disciples felt that the resurrected Jesus was truly marvelous and mysterious—suddenly He would come and suddenly He would leave; unexpectedly He would appear and unexpectedly He would disappear without any trace; yet He had a physical form. They did not understand how this could be. They were at a loss; they could not comprehend what this was all about, and they did not know what to do. This was all due to the fact that they were still ignorant concerning the Spirit, that He was now within them; and they were not clear that as the Spirit the Lord was with them and that once He came He would never leave. Sometimes the Lord would manifest His presence to them, but that was because He cared for their weakness. In this way the Lord trained them in their faith. He wanted them to know and be accustomed to His invisible presence.

To the disciples this lesson was very hard. They were already accustomed to the Lord's visible presence. When the Lord was in the flesh, they followed Him closely. They journeyed with Him, lodged with Him, and followed Him everywhere in His ministry. To them this kind of visible presence was very good; He was visible and touchable. But now He could be visible in an instant and then invisible in the next. He had resurrected, yet they could not always touch Him. Finally, one day Peter could no longer bear it. He, the head sheep of the flock, said to his brothers, "I am going fishing." They replied, "We also are coming with you." They went and got into the boat, and that night they caught nothing (John 21:2-3). Ordinarily, night is the best time for fishing, and Peter and John were experienced fishermen, but that night they caught nothing. This was because the Lord drove away all the fish by His authority. They did not catch any fish, but they did gain the Lord Jesus (v. 4).

The Lord knew that they went fishing for their livelihood; they were hungry and hoped to catch some fish for their food. "Then Jesus said to them, Little children, you do not have any fish to eat, do you? They answered Him, No. And He said to them, Cast the net on the right side of the boat, and you will find some. They cast therefore, and they were no longer able to haul it in because of the abundance of fish" (vv. 5-6). Then John said to Peter, "It is the Lord!" When Peter heard that it was the Lord, he came to his senses. Immediately he threw himself into the sea and went quickly to the Lord. Later when the disciples got out onto the land, "they saw a fire of coals laid there, and fish lying on it and bread" (vv. 7-9). They went fishing for their livelihood, yet the Lord prepared cooked fish for them. After they were fed, the Lord left without saying goodbye and disappeared.

It was in this way that the disciples were trained by the Lord for forty days. Then the Lord charged them "not to depart from Jerusalem, but to wait for the promise of the Father, which, He said,...you shall be baptized in the Holy Spirit not many days from now" (Acts 1:4-5). Following this, the Lord ascended to the heavens. *Not many days from now* refers to the feast of Pentecost which would be ten days later. The day the Lord resurrected was the Feast of the Firstfruits. Then He was with the disciples for forty days, and ten days later was the Feast of Pentecost. The disciples, after learning their lessons from the Lord for forty days, obeyed the Lord's word not to be scattered or to go fishing but to pray together in one accord for ten days. Then when the time arrived, on the day of Pentecost, the Holy Spirit came down and was poured upon them.

THE SPIRIT TODAY BEING IN US
AND ALSO POURED UPON US

I like to tell you that on that day of Pentecost God's work to save us was completely accomplished. God not only had become a man, lived the human life on earth, and died on the cross to bear our sins, but He also resurrected to become the life-giving Spirit, entered into His disciples, and poured out the Spirit. Therefore, this Spirit is the Triune God—the Holy Father, the Holy Son, and the Holy Spirit. The creating and redeeming Triune God has become the all-inclusive life-giving Spirit, who is omnipresent.

From that day to the present, for close to two thousand years, He has always been on the earth and has never left. If we read world history, we will see a remarkable thing that from Christ's ascension to the present day the name of Jesus Christ has been widely proclaimed as the gospel. For the past two thousand years war, famine, and death have occurred incessantly on this earth, and they are on the increase. However, at the same time another thing has also been happening continuously; that is, the gospel of Jesus Christ has been and still is being preached throughout the whole earth. Therefore, it is marvelous to realize that today the name of Jesus Christ and the gospel have been preached to every race and nation in every place and corner of the world. Furthermore, every believer of Jesus has the desire to preach the gospel. Another wonderful thing is that although there are oppositions to the gospel in various parts of the world, where the opposition is stronger, there the preaching of the gospel is stronger and the number of those who believe is also greater.

Why is the gospel being widely preached? Why do we, the saved ones, desire to preach the gospel? The reason is that within us we have a mysterious and unexplainable Spirit. Anyone who has this Spirit has the desire to preach the gospel. As Christians, we all have the desire to preach Jesus. We feel good when we preach Him; all our illnesses are gone and our worries are forgotten. We feel healthy mentally and physically when we talk about Jesus.

Believing in Jesus is also a wonderful thing. We are saved ones, but we cannot explain why we have believed in Jesus. Although we do not know what this is all about, we just believe in Him and love Him. All this is a story of the Spirit.

Today this Spirit is the Triune God Himself, who passed through the steps of the creation of the universe, incarnation, death, and resurrection for the accomplishment of redemption, and who also passed through ascension to become the unlimited Holy Spirit to enter into us, to be poured upon us, and to move on the whole earth. Wherever the name of Jesus is preached, He is there. His name is He Himself, His person; Jesus is His name, and His person is the Spirit. Today the Spirit comes to us whenever we call on the name of Jesus, praying to Him and praising Him. This is the story of the Spirit.

NEEDING TO DIG THE WELL
THAT THE LIVING WATER MAY FLOW

Dear brothers and sisters, simply speaking, this Spirit has already descended. The second stanza of *Hymns*, #250 says, "Christ, the Rock, is riven; / Living water's flowing." This Rock is the Lord Jesus, and the living water is the Spirit. Today the Holy Spirit is filling the whole earth. Whenever and wherever anyone would open his heart and his mouth to call, "O Lord Jesus!" there and then the Holy Spirit enters into him whether or not he knows it. This is the experience of our salvation, and this is the gospel of God. The gospel is that God created the heavens and the earth; then He became flesh and passed through death and resurrection to become the Spirit moving on the earth. When you hear the gospel and call on His name, the Spirit enters into you, and you become one spirit with the Lord. Then it is too late for you to change your mind, and you cannot give Him up even if you wanted to. Not only will He not leave you, but He will also be in you to transform you continually.

We, the saved ones, have the Spirit in us; this is an accomplished fact. Therefore, we do not need to ask again for the Spirit to come into us. Moreover, we do not need to ask for the Spirit to come upon us. What we need is to "dig the ground." To "dig the ground" is to pray and confess our sins. If we desire to be filled with the Holy Spirit, we must pray. When we pray, God, who is light, will shine on our condition and make manifest our thoughts and intentions. Then we must confess and ask the Lord to forgive us of the evil thoughts within us. This kind of confessing will cause our inner spirit to be living and strong. The problem today is that we do not pray, and as a result the "mud" piles up and obstructs the flow of the river of living water within us. Therefore, in the Old Testament types, there is not only the water flowing out of the smitten rock but also the digging of the well. When the mud is dug away, the water gushes up from the well. This is the experience we need today.

Some of the largest farm lands are in Texas. I was in Texas for a while, and I visited a special region where there is good agricultural production. The production there depends not only on the rain from heaven but also on the water drawn from the flow of water under the ground. There is a city in New Mexico which also has a large underground water flow. Part of California was a desert previously, but now all of Southern California is irrigated by the underground water drawn by electric power. This is a method of production in the southern part of the United States. In the same manner, today we do not depend on the Spirit to strengthen us from outside because the Spirit is already in us. We only need to pray, and even pray unceasingly; then the Holy Spirit will be flowing unceasingly in us. If we do not pray, we do not feel that we are dirty. The more we pray, however, the more we will see our filthiness, and the more we will then confess our sins. Just as in house cleaning, if we do it superficially, we will not see that things are very dusty, but if we do it carefully, we will see that the place is full of dust.

Stanza 3 says, "I will dig by praying, / Dig the dirt entirely, / Thus release the Spirit, / Let the stream flow freely." When we first begin to pray, we are inexperienced and awkward like those who have just learned to walk. If we practice daily, however, we will become skillful. If we do not pray, we will not become skillful, but the more we pray, the more skillful we become. To pray is to dig the well. When you first practice to pray, you may not have any feeling, but if you pray a little longer, the love toward the Lord will gush up from within you. Sometimes you will even weep because you see that although you are so wicked, the Lord loves you so much. This is the release of the Spirit. Then when you continue to pray according to the feeling within you, you have a sweet experience. If you stop praying, however, you will be like a car whose ignition is turned off and needs to be restarted. Initially you may not like to pray, but the more you practice, the more you will taste the sweetness of praying, and the more you will like to pray. This is to dig the well.

TO ABIDE IN THE LORD
REQUIRING US NOT TO QUENCH THE SPIRIT

By thus digging away all the obstructions, the living water will flow, and spontaneously we will be abiding in the Lord. First Thessalonians 5:19 says, "Do not quench the Spirit." In the Chinese Union Version this verse is translated, "Do not quench the inspiration of the Spirit." Fifty years ago when I read this verse, I felt I did not know what was meant by the inspiration of the Spirit, so how could I quench it? Gradually, I realized that the Spirit is inspiring us every moment. He is in us like the air. If we do not have air, we will die. Likewise, within us, the saved ones, is the Spirit, who inspires us every day.

Many have a mistaken understanding concerning the inspiration of the Holy Spirit. They think that the Spirit's inspiration must involve a great act or event. Actually, the inspiration of the Holy Spirit is like the movement of the air within us. We always have air within us for whatever we do; without air we would stop breathing and thus could not do anything. Likewise, in our daily living, the Holy Spirit is moving within us all the time. If instead of acting according to the Spirit's moving within, we act according to our own desire, this is to quench the inspiration of the Holy Spirit; that is, we quench the Spirit.

For instance, for the sake of the Lord's work I need to know the world situation, and therefore I read the newspapers. The content of the newspapers is a big temptation; therefore, I read only the headings to get the major points and avoid reading the rest. But some of the brothers simply like to read the newspapers; the more they read, the more they like to read, and the more they read, the more they lose the sense of the Spirit. The Spirit within them is clearly saying, "Do not read anymore," yet they keep on reading. This is to quench the Spirit. Another example is that some sisters like to go shopping and enjoy the pleasure of buying things, but they do not realize how much they quench the Spirit in such shopping trips.

The Triune God became flesh and died for us on the cross, bearing our sins; then He resurrected and became the life-giving Spirit. When we called on His name, He came to dwell in us and we were saved. This is a real fact, not a theory or philosophical doctrine. The Spirit's indwelling us is not a matter of His being high or mighty; instead, He is lowly and gentle and is often wronged by us. We often ignore Him, disregard Him, and even quench Him; yet He remains with us.

For us to abide in the Lord, the most crucial thing is to not quench the Spirit. When you talk with your wife, do not quench the Spirit. If the Spirit forbids you to continue talking, you must not reply, "Lord, let me say two more sentences, or at least let me finish this sentence." If you continue to talk on and on, you eventually will completely forget the Spirit. Although the Spirit will not leave you, you will quench the Spirit. To abide in the Lord, first of all we must not quench the Spirit.

First John 2:27 says, "The anointing which you have received from Him abides in you;...His anointing...is true and is not a lie, and even as it has taught you, abide in Him." The anointing ointment is the Spirit, and the anointing of this ointment, that is, the moving of the Spirit, never stops. You may quench Him, but He will not mind and will still keep on anointing you within. If you argue, He anoints you silently; when you calm down, He moves you again, causing you to repent and confess your sins.

For us to abide in the Lord, we must learn to not quench the Spirit at all but to cooperate with Him completely and to not argue with Him. Sisters, when you pick up an item in the department store and within you He is telling you to put it down, you should simply put it down quickly. When He tells you not to buy, you should quickly get into your car and go home. If you do this, you will not quench the Spirit or reason with Him. If you obey the Spirit, you may feel sad when you first get into your car, but when the car starts to move, you will begin to have joy and will be able to open your mouth to praise the Lord. But if you quench the Spirit and buy that item, you may be happy at that moment. When you get into your car, while driving home you will sense that you have a heavy burden and you will become sad. Upon arriving home you may consider throwing the item away, but you may feel that this is too wasteful. However, if you keep the item, you will feel that it is a bothering, and when you use it, you will have no peace at all. Eventually, you simply have to repent and confess to the Lord.

NOT TO QUENCH THE SPIRIT
BEING NOT TO NEGLECT THE LORD'S WORD

If you argue and quench the Spirit, the result will be that you cannot pray when you want to pray. You will also have no peace in your heart or have any desire to attend the church meetings. Thus, you are not abiding in the Lord. If, however, you do not quench the Spirit, you will abide in the Lord and will not neglect His words. In John 6:63 the Lord Jesus said, "The words which I have spoken to you are spirit and are life." The Lord's Spirit and the Lord's words cannot be separated.

Therefore, when you do not quench the Spirit, it means you have not neglected the Lord's words; but when you neglect the Lord's words, you quench the Spirit. These two things are one.

First Thessalonians is on the Christian's daily life, Colossians is on the life of experiencing Christ, and Ephesians is on the life of experiencing the church. To have these three kinds of lives we need to pray unceasingly and give thanks in everything. Not only so, Colossians tells us that a life of experiencing Christ depends on our letting the word of the Lord dwell in us richly (Col. 3:16); Ephesians says that for us to have the church life, we must be filled in spirit (Eph. 5:18b). When we have the Spirit of God filling our spirit within and the word of the Lord dwelling in us, spontaneously we can give thanks at all times for all things.

According to 1 Thessalonians, if we are unable to give thanks, it is because we have quenched the Spirit and neglected the prophecies (5:18-20). Prophecies are the words given by the Spirit, which are also the words of the Lord. The Bible is the Lord's word in written form, and the prophecies are the Lord's speaking in us. Therefore, *do not quench the Spirit* and *do not despise prophecies* mean *do not quench the Spirit of God* and *do not neglect the words of the Lord*. We have the Spirit, and often we also have the instant words of the Lord within us. If we quench the Spirit and neglect the words of the Lord, we will come out of the Lord. But if we neither quench the Spirit nor neglect the instant words of the Lord, we will abide in the Lord. When we abide in the Lord, spontaneously we can exercise our spirit, pray, and give thanks in everything. This is a practical way for us to abide in the Lord.

CHAPTER FIVE

NOT A MATTER OF SIN BUT A MATTER OF "I"

Scripture Reading: John 6:57; Gal. 2:20; 1 Cor. 15:10; Phil. 1:20b-21a

The title of this message is *Not a Matter of Sin but a Matter of "I."* This statement does not sound Chinese, nor does it sound like a word from the Bible. However, according to my personal experience, if you want to abide in the Lord and enjoy His life, you must understand that this is not a matter of whether you sin but of whether it is you who live. If it is you who live, then even if you do not sin, you are still abiding in yourself. When it is not you who live, you are blessed.

ABIDING IN THE LORD
NOT BEING A MATTER OF SINNING

Even if I do not sin and I am a "saint" today, I am still "I" without any change. Then this "I" will be the root of trouble. As long as "I" am here, there will be trouble. If we see this point clearly, we will abide in the Lord even when we would not like to. If it is that you merely do not sin, it is highly possible that you are still one hundred percent in yourself. In other words, while you may not sin, it is still possible that you are one hundred percent not abiding in the Lord. To abide in the Lord is not a matter of whether or not one commits sin. Of course, when one abides in the Lord, he cannot sin. However, not committing sin is not equal to abiding in the Lord.

Confucius never heard about Christ or knew the Lord, yet he could say, "One cannot pray when he sins against heaven." He did not know anything regarding the Lord, but his ethical speech and ways were commendable. He was truly a perfect man. At the age of seventy he was able to do the desires of his heart yet not transgress what was right; that is, he did not sin. Notwithstanding, he did not abide in the Lord and had nothing to do with the Lord. This is strong proof that abiding in the Lord is altogether not a matter of sinning or not sinning.

REPENTANCE BEING A CHANGE OF MIND

As natural beings we have our natural concepts from birth. Thus, when we hear the Lord's word and the gospel of God, we remember our sins. Of course, this is right. With regard to the gospel of God, our sins certainly are a problem. Therefore, all those who preach the gospel always ask people to repent, and also the people themselves realize that they are sinful and consequently need to repent. However, this kind of realization is too natural. According to the light of the gospel truth, a so-called sinless person also needs repentance. In Greek, the meaning of *repent* is not mainly on repentance. It is not that you have sinned and made mistakes, so you regret and correct yourself by making a turn. Rather, it is that you have done something which may not have had anything to do with sinning, but afterward you still regret and correct yourself by making a turn. For example, sometimes the sisters repent after going to a store to do some shopping, even though shopping itself is something apart from sinning. The Greek word for *repent* is composed of two parts: one part implies "change" and the other part means "mind." The combination of the two means "a change of mind." Therefore, to repent is to have a change of mind, issuing in regret. It is to have a turn in purpose.

GOD CREATING MAN WITH THE PURPOSE THAT MAN MIGHT TAKE GOD AS HIS CONTENT AND THEREBY EXPRESS GOD

To repent means to cause our mind, which was going the wrong way, to turn around. Due to our misconceptions, we think that morality is our goal and is the meaning of our human life. However, the divine revelation in the Bible shows us that God is man's goal, man's center, and man's meaning. God should be his content. The Bible does not say that God created man according to the image of morality. Rather, it says that God created man according to the image of God. This means that God created man that man may express God. For man to express God, he must have God as his content. If we do not have God within us, there is no way for us to express God. What is expressed outwardly altogether depends on what has been formed within. Therefore, it is not a matter of morality but a matter of God.

When man fell, he fell into sin. Confucius and Mencius also were born among fallen men. Hence, their concept was that man needs improvement from a fallen condition to a moral condition. Because they did not know God, they tried to change man altogether by teaching benevolence and justice according to their moral concepts. This is the work of Confucius and Mencius: teaching morality and, in particular, benevolence and justice. However, the Bible reveals that God is the source and that He created man for His own purpose, that is, that man might be filled with God, take God as life, and have God as his content for the expression of God.

MAN'S NATURAL CONCEPT
BEING TO DO EVERYTHING BY HIMSELF

When I was first saved, I heard about abiding in the Lord. My concept was that from morning to evening I should not lose my temper, I should always be gentle toward others, I should speak at a slow pace and with a moderate tone, I should not do things in haste, and I should walk neither too fast nor too slow and make no loud sound. At that time the books in the Bible I liked to read the most were James and Proverbs. All typical Chinese appreciate the book of Proverbs. Therefore, the Chinese New Testament is printed with Proverbs as an appendix. The book of James resembles Proverbs. James says, "But let every man be quick to hear, slow to speak, slow to wrath" (1:19). The elderly James truly was experienced. To only listen and not speak means that one could never get angry. The best way for an angry person to control his anger is to keep his mouth shut. No matter how much others may offend you, if you simply hold on to this secret of keeping your mouth shut, you will not get angry.

However, once you open your mouth and the words start to flow out, your wrath will be released. Therefore, I totally agreed with what James said, and I even practiced this at times.

Later I discovered that what I was practicing was neither abiding in the Lord nor enjoying the Lord's life. I misunderstood its meaning. As a result I practiced many years yet had no success. The Bible says that when the Lord was suffering persecution, He was "like a lamb that is led to the slaughter / And like a sheep that is dumb before its shearers" (Isa. 53:7). He was truly like a sheep. To abide in the Lord is to be like a sheep, but I was like a fast horse. How can I be a sheep? Therefore, although I fully believed in the Lord, never doubted, and behaved as a Christian, I was often discouraged because I felt that I could not make it. For a period of time I was very disappointed. Still I continued to practice and learn slowly.

What I am fellowshipping with you is based not only upon the Bible but also upon what I have learned. Perhaps some would say that the title of this message is very strange. This is so, but it is through experience that I know the truth which I speak. According to what was taught in the past, if we truly want to practice abiding in the Lord, we should rise up early, pray first, then wash, and then sit down to read the Word. However, I can guarantee that you might be able to practice this for three days, but you will not be able to continue it for thirty days. Maybe you can do it for even thirty days, but you will not be able to carry it out for three months. I myself have practiced this way of rising up early to pray and read the Bible, perhaps more than all of you. The first two days I would do well, but it did not last, and I could not continue.

Finally, I came to realize that it is not a matter of practicing certain things, not a matter of sinning or not sinning, not a matter of having morning revival or not having morning revival, and not a matter of praying first after getting out of bed. I discovered that even though I practiced all these things, I was still "I," and I remained unchanged. It was I who prayed before washing, and it was definitely I who read the Word after praying. Although outwardly I did many things, inwardly it was still I.

Although I continue to encourage you about things—because people need encouragement and cannot do well without it—I know that in the end all encouragement will not avail. At the most you will be burning only for five minutes. Not only so, even with us Christians who love the Lord and who are zealous for Him, our zeal often does not last for more than five days. Therefore, many times before five days are up, we have to change our "gimmick." In the practice of the church life, the elders often change their gimmick, perhaps every five months, because no gimmick can last from the beginning of the year to the end. Whatever practice we try to maintain, eventually our zeal for it will diminish. The reason for this is that I am still "I."

NO LONGER I WHO LIVE,
BUT CHRIST WHO LIVES IN ME

Galatians 2:20 says, "It is no longer I who live, but it is Christ who lives in me." Religion, ethics, or any kind of philosophical concept requires us to become perfect people who are without sins or transgressions. Only the biblical concept is superior to the human concept; its highest goal is not for man to be a perfect man without any sin or transgression, but for man to live God's life that God may live in man. Such a concept is clearly revealed in Galatians 2:20.

"I am crucified with Christ." We have already pointed out that the meaning of crucifixion is not suffering but termination. However, most Christians have the wrong understanding—that to take up the cross is to suffer. This is altogether a natural concept and not the pure revelation of the Bible. The cross referred to in the Bible is not for us to suffer but for us to be terminated. In John 19:15 when the Jews pointed to the Lord Jesus who was standing before Pilate and said, "Crucify Him," what they meant was, "Get rid of Him." Their purpose for putting the Lord on the cross was not that He would suffer but that they would get rid of Him.

The meaning of "I am crucified with Christ" is that in Christ I have been annihilated, terminated, together with

Him. Whether I am good or bad, I have been terminated. Whether I am moral or immoral, I have been terminated. Whether I hate or love others, I have been terminated. Moreover, whether I disobey my parents or honor them, I have been terminated. Paul, the one who wrote this word, said that before he was saved, before he received Christ, he became blameless "as to the righteousness which is in the law" (Phil. 3:6). He could be considered a perfect man according to the law. Nevertheless, he still repented. Humanly speaking, he was proven to be one who was truly blameless, a perfect man, without sin or transgression; but such a man was still not what God wants. It was not until after Paul repented that he could say that it was not the righteousness of the law that would be manifested in his body, but as always Christ would be magnified in his body, whether through life or through death (Phil. 1:20b). The rendering of *as always* is very meaningful. It is not a short-lived matter but *always*. Paul did not magnify Christ in a short-lived way like the night-blooming flowers which are beautiful for a moment but wither at the blink of an eye. Rather, he always magnified Christ whether through life or through death. Instead of ethics, it was Christ who was magnified in his body. He said, "For to me, to live is Christ" (v. 21a).

Dear brothers and sisters, we all need to see that we are very much governed by our natural concepts. Each time we read the Bible, we bring in our natural concepts. Every time we speak about abiding in the Lord, we think that this refers to being blameless, to sinless perfection. We think that to abide in the Lord is to be a perfect person. Actually this is not so. To abide in the Lord means that in all things it is not you who are doing and living, but it is the Lord who is doing and living. In my life I have had many experiences, but what I have experienced the most is that when we Christians do not live by the Lord but by ourselves, that is the most dangerous moment. Any time you live by yourself, you may feel very good and that you do not have any problems, but actually this is the most dangerous time.

I often say that you can never hate those whom you did not once love. You would not bother to hate the people on the streets whom you do not know and who are not related to you. Have you ever hated anyone whom you did not love previously? In like manner, those who have the worst temper are not those who easily lose their temper. Those who frequently lose their temper are in the habit of losing their temper, so they do not readily go into a rage. Rather, it is those who are very gentle, who are the most like lambs, that when they explode with anger, they become altogether uncontrollable. Why is this? This is because they have been living by the self. If you love by your self and you are gentle by your self, eventually, you will hate by your self and explode with anger by your self.

The Bible tells us at the outset that there were two trees in the garden of Eden: the tree of life and the tree of the knowledge of good and evil. The tree of the knowledge of good and evil comprises not only the knowledge of good but also the knowledge of evil. Good and evil are joined together; they are of the same nature. Where there is good, there is also evil; evil always accompanies good. This is the truth in the Bible. When good comes, evil will certainly follow. For example, the date trees in North China have thorns. If there are dates, there are thorns. There is not one tree that bears dates that is without thorns. In the same way, evil always comes with good.

A certain Christian said that if you have the knowledge of evil, actually that knowledge is sin. It would be best that in our thoughts and in our concepts there is no such thing as sin, for then it is guaranteed that we will not sin. If we know both good and evil, the result will be that we do both good and evil. However, the Bible does not tell us to get rid of evil and to do good. The Bible tells us to live wholly by the Lord. When we live by the Lord, not only will we not hate others, but we will also not love others in ourselves. We will simply live by the Lord.

HE WHO EATS THE LORD
LIVING BECAUSE OF THE LORD

The Lord Jesus said in John 6:57, "So he who eats Me, he also shall live because of Me." What does *because of* Me mean? To say that it means "by" may seem quite correct, but in

Greek the word is not *by* but a word that is hard to interpret. Even the best expositors have not fully explained it. Experience is required to understand this. To explain this word, we need the entire Gospel of John.

The Lord Jesus said, "As the living Father has sent Me and I live because of the Father, so he who eats Me, he also shall live because of Me" (v. 57). The living Father sent the Lord Jesus. This sending is not the sending in its ordinary sense, in that the sender stays back while the sent one goes forth. For example, if you have difficulty in getting around, you may send someone to get a book for you. This kind of sending means that you do not move, while the sent one moves. However, the Gospel of John tells us that when the Father God sent the Lord Jesus, the Father God came with and in the Lord Jesus. When the Father God sent the Son, He first entered into the Son, and then He sent the Son. The Father lives, and He lives in the Son. The Father's living in the Son sends the Son. Hence, the Son as the sent One lives because there is One living in Him.

In John 6:57 the word *because* means that in the Son there is a living God and that His being and His living are the cause, or the reason, of the Son's living. Therefore, this verse means that the living Father entered the Son and lived in the Son, and then He sent the Son. When the Father moved, the Son moved; when the Father spoke, the Son spoke. Whatever the Son spoke or did was because of the Father's speaking and doing in Him. Thus, the living Father is the factor of the Son's living and moving. The living Father lived in the Son and sent the Son; hence, the Son lived because of the Father's living in Him, and the Son spoke and moved because of the Father's speaking and moving in Him.

In the same way, those who eat the Lord will live because of the Lord. To eat is to take food into us as our life supply. Thus, to eat the Lord Jesus is to take the Lord Jesus into us as our life supply. This Lord Jesus is also living. He always lives in us; He lives in us daily, and He lives in us unceasingly. We are those who have received the Lord Jesus, so we should live because He lives in us. We live and move because the living Lord Jesus lives and moves in us. He who eats the Lord has the living Lord living within him. Thus, this living Lord is the factor of his living, as Paul said, "It is no longer I who live, but it is Christ who lives in me." Christ lives in me as the factor of my living. Because He lives like this in me, I live. Therefore, when I live, actually it is not I who live but it is Christ who lives.

NEEDING TO PRACTICE IN OUR DAILY LIVING

While this truth is very difficult to explain, it is still possible to speak it rather clearly. The hardest thing, however, is to apply this truth to our daily living. The young people are full of energy; therefore, it is difficult for them to deny themselves in all things and live by the Lord. The older people tend to boast of their age and despise others. The older they are, the more they think they are experienced; thus, it is even harder for them to deny themselves and live by the Lord. In addition, in great matters or in difficult times it is easier for us to live by the Lord, but in the small things in our daily life it is very easy for us to depend on ourselves. Nevertheless, as those who love the Lord we should ask ourselves, "Is it I who live or is it the Lord who lives today?" I have many children and grandchildren, and every time I have contact with them I experience a strong correction within: "Is this you or the Lord Jesus? Is this the Lord speaking in you or is it you yourself?"

It is not a matter of being right or wrong but a matter of whether or not it is the Lord. If you are speaking or behaving in yourself, then what you might think is right is still wrong. If you live by the Lord, then even some things you think are wrong are right. The revelation in the four Gospels is clear; the Lord healed the sick on the Sabbath. The Pharisees said that He violated the Sabbath, but the Lord said that He was not wrong because He is the Lord, He is God. As the One who established the Sabbath, He had the authority to put the Sabbath aside. Eventually, He said that the Son of Man was the Lord of the Sabbath. He had the authority to establish it and the authority to abolish it. Hence, we should all let the Lord be the Lord. He is the Lord; whatever He does is right. If we do it, everything is wrong because it is not what the Lord wants. The Lord does not want us to do anything. What he wants is to be in us and to live out Himself from within us.

This kind of concept is easy to understand but not easy to practice. We love the Lord very much and are willing to live by the Lord, but whenever we do anything, we always live ourselves. We have all received the mercy of the Lord to at least not do sinful things. In the matters in our daily life, however, especially in small things, it is very easy for us to live completely by ourselves and not by the Lord. It is not until the meeting time that we might remember we should go to the meetings by the Lord.

Even in the meetings we may still not live by the Lord. When you should open your mouth, you would not. The Lord urges you to praise, prophesy, or pray, yet you are often afraid and unwilling to lose face. You might feel that when you have learned to speak and can be an instant sensation, then you will be willing to open your mouth. Therefore, it is still you who live. If you truly live by the Lord, when you have the inner sense to pray, you will not care whether it sounds good or bad; you will pray. Thus, whether it is in our daily life or in the meetings, we do not live by the Lord. Whether we are newly saved or we have been saved for many years, all of us are good at living ourselves.

On the cross the Lord Jesus was a Lamb. Instead of threatening people, He was mistreated by them. After His resurrection from the dead, He became a dove. Even we often mistreat our Lord Jesus. Nevertheless, He is patient as a dove. He moves continually within us so that we would not do anything by ourselves but instead allow Him to do everything. Just as He lived because of the Father, He also wants us to be transformed into His image and live because of Him. We thank the Lord that due to His infusion and influence, even though we often live by ourselves, we do have a measure of His image. Whether we are shepherding others or going to work or school, we all need to ask for the Lord's leading and to live by the Lord. Whenever you do not live by the Lord, even if you do good, you are still outside of the Lord and not abiding in the Lord. This is not doctrine; this is a matter of actual practice and experience. May we all be able to practice so that in every action, word, and attitude we would entirely live by the Lord and live because of the Lord. Whether in speech or action, we must live by His speaking and moving in us. He must be the factor in what we speak and what we do.

In the same principle, we love the brothers and sisters because He is in us loving them. His love in us is the factor of our love. We love the brothers and sisters because He loves them. It is not that He loves whom He loves, and we love whom we love. It is not because He loves, so in like manner we love. Rather, it is because the Lord loves in us that we love together with Him. This is to live by the Lord. The result is that we will live in the Lord and abide in the Lord. Spontaneously, we will also enjoy the Lord as our life. May the Lord have mercy on us and grant us the grace so that we all can practice this.

CHAPTER SIX

IN THE HOLIEST PLACE, LIVE WITHIN THE VEIL

Scripture Reading: Heb. 10:19-20; 4:16; 1 Cor. 3:16; 1 Thes. 5:23

Prayer: O Lord, we worship You that You have gathered us before You, and we believe that You are with us. How good it is that we can be here around Your word, and by this we can draw near to You and contact You as the Spirit! O Lord, we really thank You that, as our Savior, You died on the cross for our sins, You bore all our offenses, You were judged by God for us, and You were raised from the dead. O Lord, cleanse us with Your precious blood. By this blood we have the boldness to enter into the Holy of Holies. Lord, we have no fear within us because our conscience has been purified by being sprinkled with the precious blood. Having peace and boldness before You, we can hear Your speaking.

Lord, we pray that You reach every one of us and visit each one. Come into us to touch our heart again, and open up our spirit and the understanding of our mind that we may have the wisdom to understand Your word and may also have the revelation to see Your vision. O Lord, cause us all to be moved by You in our spirit to receive Your grace. Cause us all to know You as the true and living God and as the all-inclusive Spirit, who is in our mouth and in our heart for us to contact at any time.

Lord, we believe that Your Spirit is with us. We praise You that You have made us Your temple; we are Your dwelling place. We and You as two spirits have become one spirit. We pray that You bless us for us to have You as our life, even abundantly. Lord, grant us the utterance and give us the fresh and clear word to meet the need of the people. We also pray that Your word, bringing with it Your authority, Your power, and Yourself, would come to people to subdue them that they may repent to You, turn back to You, and see the corruption of the world and the vanity of human life. O Lord, we also ask You to shine upon us so that we may truly know You. Even more, we ask You to bestow Your blessing upon us that we may all have life and may have it abundantly. Amen.

THE HOLIEST PLACE, THE VEIL, AND THE THRONE OF GRACE

The title of this message is *In the Holiest Place, Live within the Veil.* This is taken from a line of the second stanza of Hymn #557 in the Chinese *Hymns.* The Bible speaks of the Holiest Place and the veil. However, Christians in general probably do not know the meaning of the phrase *the Holiest Place.* In addition, they explain the word *veil* merely as a curtain used to separate spaces or things, and they know even less what *within the veil* refers to.

After I was saved, I was puzzled about what the Holiest Place was and what *within the veil* meant. I felt that it was not too hard to understand these two words—*Holiest* and *grace.* But *Holiest* plus *place* equaling the Holiest Place referred to a location. What kind of place was this? Furthermore, *grace* plus *throne* equaled the throne of grace. What kind of throne was this? On earth there is a great mess everywhere. Where is the Holiest Place? And where can the throne of grace be? It seemed that it was not easy to find them. Therefore, I concluded that the Holiest Place and the throne of grace must be in the "heavenly hall." Thus, "In the Holiest Place, touch the throne of grace" must refer to our entering into the "heavenly hall." Moreover, the expression *heavenly hall* is definitely found in Hebrews 9:24 in the Chinese Union Version, but in reality, *heavenly hall,* which is altogether a Buddhist term borrowed by the Chinese Bible translators, does not correspond with the teaching of the Scriptures. The term *heavenly hall* does not exist either in the Hebrew text of the Old Testament or in the Greek text of the New Testament.

In order to understand the meaning of these terms—*the Holiest Place, the throne of grace,* and *within the veil*—I went to many places to listen to sermons for many years. However, it was not easy to hear messages concerning these things in the common Christian meetings. It was not until one day when I went to the meetings of a Brethren Assembly that I heard an explanation of what the Holiest Place is, what the throne of grace is, and what it is to be within the veil. At that time, they had prayer meetings every Tuesday night. During the meeting, the whole congregation would kneel down and pray with loud groanings. They said that this is to "enter the Holy of Holies" and "come forward to the throne of grace." Afterward I found out that these phrases were quoted from Hebrews 10:19-20 and 4:16. I received a great deal of help from them. After I had had a considerable amount of experience, I gradually understood the real meaning of "entering the Holy of Holies" and "coming forward to the throne of grace."

THE TYPES OF THE TABERNACLE AND
THE HOLY OF HOLIES IN THE OLD TESTAMENT

In the Old Testament, when the Israelites came out of Egypt and journeyed through the wilderness, God commanded Moses to build a tabernacle for Him so that He could be with the children of Israel. Outside of this tabernacle was the outer court, which was one hundred cubits in length, fifty cubits in width, and enclosed with the fine linen as the curtains. The tabernacle itself was thirty cubits in length, ten cubits in width, and ten cubits in height. It was divided into two parts: the Holy Place and the Holiest Place. The Holy Place was twenty cubits in length and the Holiest Place was ten cubits in length. This tabernacle was the dwelling place of God among His redeemed people at that time on the earth. It was also the precursor of the temple; first there was the tabernacle, and then it became the temple. When the Israelites were wandering in the wilderness, the tabernacle was the dwelling place of God. After they entered into the good land, Canaan, and settled down there, they built a fixed tabernacle of stones, and that was the holy temple. The contents of the temple were the same as that of the tabernacle, having three parts: the outer court, the Holy Place, and the Holiest Place.

To enter the Holy of Holies, the priests had to first pass through the gate of the outer court which was on the east toward the sunrise. Then they passed through the outer court into the Holy Place and then finally into the Holiest Place. At the entrance of the tabernacle in the outer court there was the altar of burnt offering, where they offered sacrifices to God. In between the Holy Place and the Holiest Place, there was a very thick veil separating the two. The common people could enter the outer court but not the Holy Place. Only the priests were qualified to enter the Holy Place. As to the Holiest Place, only the high priest, who had the highest office among the priests, was allowed to enter it once a year.

In the Holiest Place was the ark, within which were the Ten Commandments which God had established with His people. Upon the ark was a cover of pure gold with two cherubim expressing God's glory. This cover was the throne of grace. When the high priest entered the Holiest Place, the first thing he did was to sprinkle on this cover the propitiating blood from the altar to make propitiation before God for the sins of the people. It was on this cover that God forgave the sins of the people; it was also here that God fellowshipped and spoke with the high priest. Because this cover was sprinkled with the propitiating blood and had there the cherubim as God's expression and was the place where God spoke to the high priest, it was called the throne of grace, the place for God to give grace to man.

Therefore, we can see that the Holiest Place was the innermost part of the tabernacle, and its main content was the throne of grace, where God met with His redeemed people, forgave His people, and spoke to His people. It was here that God gave grace to people. Hence, this was truly a great matter. In this vast universe there is a small earth. On this earth there was a place called the outer court. Within the outer court there was a tabernacle, the outer part of which was the Holy Place and the inner part of which was the Holiest Place. Furthermore, within the Holiest Place there was an ark. Upon this ark there was a cover where God gave grace to man; hence, it was called the throne of grace. The throne of grace was the center of the Holiest Place.

THE FULFILLMENT AND REALITY
IN THE NEW TESTAMENT

In Hebrews 9 the apostle Paul indicates that the first tabernacle, the Holy Place, signifies the old covenant and that the second tabernacle, the Holy of Holies or the Holiest Place, signifies the new covenant (vv. 8-10). He also indicates that the Holy of Holies today is in heaven, where the Lord Jesus is (vv. 12, 24). How then can we enter into the Holy of Holies in heaven while we are still on earth? The secret is our spirit, referred to in Hebrews 4:12. The very Christ who is now in heaven is also at the same time in our spirit (Rom. 8:34, 10; 2 Tim. 4:22). As the heavenly ladder (Gen. 28:12; John 1:51) He joins our spirit to heaven and brings heaven into our spirit. Hence, whenever we turn to our spirit, we enter into the Holy of Holies. There we meet with God, who is on the throne of grace (Heb. 4:16).

The veil which closed off the Holy of Holies typifies the flesh of Christ. When Christ's flesh was crucified, this veil was split in two from top to bottom (Matt. 27:51), thus opening a new and living way (Heb. 10:19-20) for those of us who were alienated from God, who is signified by the tree of life (Gen. 3:22-24), to enter into the Holy of Holies—into our spirit—to contact and enjoy God as our life and life supply.

The first stanza of Hymn #770 says, "In the holiest place, touch the throne of grace, / Grace as a river shall flow." This is what Revelation 22:1 says: There is "a river of water of life, bright as crystal, proceeding out of the throne of God and of the Lamb in the middle of its street." That throne of God is the throne of grace. Whenever we come to the throne of grace, the grace of God is like a river flowing to us.

DWELLING IN THE HOLIEST PLACE
AND LIVING WITHIN THE VEIL

Hymns, #551 is a Pentecostal hymn. In the last century, a group of Christians felt that Christianity was too dead and deadening and that it had fallen into rituals and letters and was short of the Spirit and life. From their study of the Word they saw that at the apostles' time, on the day of Pentecost, the Holy Spirit was poured out upon people. Therefore, a group of Christians in England began to pray and seek for the Holy Spirit. They testified that they prayed to such an extent that they also received the outpouring of the Holy Spirit. This was the start of the Pentecostal movement.

The Pentecostal movement developed and spread to the United States in the beginning of the twentieth century. It first prevailed in Massachusetts and then continued on to the West until it reached the Los Angeles area. At the same time, a group of Christians in a certain place in Pennsylvania on the East Coast claimed that they had received the so-called gifts of the Holy Spirit. Thus, based on the account in Exodus 15, they called the place where they were Elim (v. 27), indicating that they were not dry but rather full of the living water. Those who met there wrote this hymn. Then in 1934 this song spread to China and reached our hands. In October of the same year, Brother Watchman Nee had an Overcomers' Conference in Hangchow. Because this hymn could stir up our spirit very much, he asked me to translate the chorus into Chinese, and we sang it in the meetings.

In 1963 and 1964, when we were preparing the English hymnal, we selected the entire hymn. Then in 1966 and 1967, when we were recompiling the Chinese hymnal, we translated the entire hymn into Chinese. The first stanza of this hymn says,

> I've believed the true report,
>   Hallelujah to the Lamb!
> I have passed the outer court,
>   O glory be to God!
> I am all on Jesus' side,
> On the altar sanctified,
> To the world and sin I've died,
>   Hallelujah to the Lamb!

The third stanza says,

> I have passed the outer veil,
>   Hallelujah to the Lamb!
> Which did once God's light conceal,
>   O glory be to God!
> But the blood has brought me in

> To God's holiness so clean,
> Where there's death to self and sin,
> Hallelujah to the Lamb!

The outer court here typifies the world. Here it says that we should forsake the world instead of remaining in it. We need to be sanctified on the altar so that we can pass from the outer court through the first veil into the Holy Place, where there is the showbread table as our divine and all-inclusive supply.

The fourth stanza says,

> I'm within the holiest pale,
> Hallelujah to the Lamb!
> I have passed the inner veil,
> O glory be to God!
> I am sanctified to God
> By the power of the blood,
> Now the Lord is my abode,
> Hallelujah to the Lamb!

The inner veil typifies our self, the fallen man, and the flesh of sin put on by the Lord Jesus (Rom. 8:3). When the Lord Jesus was crucified and died, the veil of the temple was split in two from top to bottom (Matt. 27:51). This indicates that when the Lord Jesus died on the cross, our fallen man, our natural man, was also crucified there. This abolished our self, which is what separates us from God, in order that we may have an open way into the Holy of Holies to contact and enjoy God. Thus, not only God dwells in the Holy of Holies, but we also dwell in the Holy of Holies.

Stanza two says,

> I'm a king and priest to God,
> Hallelujah to the Lamb!
> By the cleansing of the blood,
> O glory be to God!
> By the Spirit's pow'r and light,
> I am living day and night,
> In the holiest place so bright,
> Hallelujah to the Lamb!

This is a description of "dwelling in the Holiest Place and living within the veil."

According to our Christian experience, the Holy of Holies today refers to our spirit. First Corinthians 3:16 says, "Do you not know that you are the temple of God, and that the Spirit of God dwells in you?" Today we are God's temple. The temple of God has three parts: the outer court, the Holy Place, and the Holy of Holies. First Thessalonians 5:23 says that as the temple of God we also have three parts: body, soul, and spirit. The body, which is the outward appearance, typifies the outer court; the soul, which is within the body, typifies the Holy Place; and the spirit, which is enveloped by the soul, typifies the Holy of Holies.

Only the saved ones can be the temple of God, because the temple of God is the dwelling place of God, the place in which God dwells. The unsaved ones do not have God dwelling in them; hence, they are not the temple of God. We all have God's indwelling. Today He is the Spirit dwelling in our spirit. In the Old Testament God dwelt in the Holy of Holies of the temple. In the New Testament God also dwells in the Holy of Holies—our spirit. Therefore, Romans 8:16 says, "The Spirit Himself witnesses with our spirit." This proves that God dwells in our spirit.

Today this God who is above all dwells in our spirit! This is tremendous. If the President wanted to come and stay in our home, we would all be surprised to receive such a great honor and would treat him as a distinguished guest. How much greater God is than the President, yet He comes to dwell in our spirit! How wonderful this is! When God dwells in us, our spirit becomes the Holy of Holies. Because the presence of God is in the Holy of Holies, the throne of grace is there. The throne of grace indicates the presence of God, which is God Himself. God comes into our spirit to give grace to us.

ABIDING IN THE LORD AND ENJOYING HIS LIFE
BY ENTERING INTO THE HOLY OF HOLIES
TO TOUCH THE THRONE OF GRACE

What does it mean to abide in the Lord and enjoy His life? First, we must know where this Lord is whom we want to enjoy. Today the Lord is in our spirit. When I was young, I felt that this matter of abiding in the Lord was very abstract. Every time I prayed, I would kneel down in a definite and sincere way. While I prayed, I would think that the Lord must be sitting high above in heaven, and hopefully my prayers would be able to reach that high. I believed the Lord could bring my prayers from the earth to heaven far above. But sometimes I did not have the assurance that my prayer would reach heaven and be heard by God. That was my condition sixty years ago.

Praise the Lord, we who are in the church today are blessed! We all know that the Lord as the Spirit comes into our spirit when we believe into Him. The Lord, who is the God who created the universe, became flesh to be a man named Jesus Christ two thousand years ago. For our redemption He went to the cross to die and bear our sins, and as the last Adam He resurrected to become the life-giving Spirit. Now He is everywhere just like the air. Romans 10 says that while we are preaching the gospel, this Spirit is with us reaching the listeners to be in their mouth and even to get into their heart. If anyone would open his heart and call, "O Lord Jesus!" the Lord as the Spirit will enter into him.

Once the Lord comes into us, He will never leave us. Sometimes we feel that it is good to believe in the Lord, but sometimes it is troublesome, since many things become inconvenient because of the Lord. However, the salvation of the Lord is truly wonderful. He not only redeems us but also comes into our spirit. Regretfully, today many Christians do not know the mystery of the salvation they have received. How blessed we are that we can know this mystery! Our Lord, who is the Lord of the universe, was undefinable and hard to find. However, because of His mercy, He became flesh and was crucified for us. Then He resurrected to become the Spirit to dwell in the spirit of those who believe in Him, and He takes up His residence in them.

To know is one thing, but to enjoy is another. This phrase, *enjoying Christ,* was used first by us. The way to enjoy Christ is, "In the Holiest Place, live within the veil." We have already pointed out that the outer court signifies our body, the Holy

Place signifies our soul, and the Holiest Place signifies our spirit. To enjoy Christ, instead of living in our soul or our body we should enter into our spirit and live in our spirit.

For example, if you get angry and quarrel with others, your body, in particular your mouth, becomes a venting organ. If you shut your mouth, you become "deflated" and your anger dissipates. However, if you continue to open your mouth, the result is that the quarreling becomes more and more serious. The more you speak, the more you feel in your soul that you are right, and eventually you even act in your flesh. At this time, instead of living in the Holy Place, you are living in the outer court.

When you live in the outer court, you must be warned by this hymn, "I've believed the true report, / Hallelujah to the Lamb! / I have passed the outer court, / O glory be to God!" You should not quarrel any more, because your flesh has been crucified with Christ. Perhaps you feel that if you do not quarrel and give vent to your anger, your heart will not be at ease and your stomach will also hurt. However, we all need to be reminded that it is best not to use our body, which is the outer court, as the instrument for quarreling and getting angry. Sometimes we have passed the outer court—not using our body as an instrument of the flesh—yet our soul, including our mind, emotion, and will, which is the part that employs our body as an instrument, is still very active and is constantly instigating us to go out again to the outer court. As a result, although we exercise control of ourselves to not live in our flesh, we are altogether living in our soul. We try to restrain ourselves from living in the flesh, but the result is that we live completely in our soul, and we become so active that we are unable to calm down.

It may be that at times like this the Lord has mercy on us and comes to remind us, saying, "Do you not know that your body is a temple of the Holy Spirit?" (1 Cor. 6:19). We belong to the Lord, and the Lord lives in us. If we receive the reminder and turn from our soul to our spirit, we enter into the Holy of Holies. Once we enter into the Holy of Holies, we enter into a refuge and reach a safe region. In this way we are preserved.

We all have this kind of experience. Every time we turn to our spirit, we repent and confess to the Lord, admitting that we live so much in the flesh and in the soul. The more we ask for the Lord's forgiveness and pray to fellowship with the Lord, the more we receive grace. Grace begins to flow to us like a river. This means that we have touched the throne of grace. If we do this, the living water saturates us and fills us until it overflows so that we are completely in grace.

At the same time, the glory of God shines through our whole being so that we have no place to hide. This leads us to see our filthiness, to see that we have wronged our spouse and our relatives and that we are wrong in many different things. Then we beat our chest, weep, and repent. In this way of confessing we receive grace immensely. This is to pass through the outer court and the Holy Place into the Holy of Holies to touch the throne of grace. The more we touch the throne of grace, the more we have the presence of God. The more we touch the throne of grace, the more we have the riches of God. Moreover, we are able to enjoy the hidden manna within the ark and have a deeper experience of Christ as the life supply. In this way we abide in the Lord and enjoy Him as our life.

CHAPTER SEVEN

EXPERIENCING THE CLEANSING OF THE LORD'S BLOOD AND ENJOYING THE ANOINTING OF THE HOLY OINTMENT

Scripture Reading: 1 John 1:6-10; 2:20, 27; Lev. 14:14-18

In this message we will go on to see another aspect of abiding in the Lord and enjoying His life, that is, experiencing the cleansing of the blood and enjoying the anointing of the ointment.

THE PRECIOUS BLOOD AND THE HOLY OINTMENT

The Precious Blood Cleansing Us from Sin

The main items in the first two chapters of 1 John are the Lord's blood and the holy ointment. The Lord's blood is for the cleansing of our sin, and our sin is of two aspects: the inward sin, the sin within us, in our heart; and the outward sins, the sins in our actions. The inward sin is our sinful nature that we have from birth. Adam fell, and sin entered into him. As the descendants of Adam, we were born with a sinful nature (Rom. 5:12). No one needs to go through a training after birth to learn how to commit sin; everyone sins naturally.

Sinning comes from human nature, from the fall. Just as a bad tree does not need to bear bad fruit to become a bad tree, so man does not need to commit sin intentionally to become a sinner. In God's eyes, human beings sin every day. Man's entire being is altogether a lie, and every part of him is a lie. The eyes can lie, the nose can lie, and even the hair can lie; sometimes even his gestures are lies. This is because the human life is a lying life. A bad tree automatically bears bad fruit without being taught, and a good tree naturally bears good fruit also without being taught. In the same way, because our nature is sinful, whatever we do, without any special intention, is naturally sinful. Inwardly we have the sinful nature, and outwardly we have the sinful actions, which are the sinful deeds. The precious blood cleanses us from our sinful nature inwardly and our sinful deeds outwardly. This is the efficacy of the precious blood.

The Efficacy of the Holy Ointment

The other item is the holy ointment. The holy ointment here does not refer to the ointment itself or to its essence; it refers to the anointing of the ointment. The English word *anointing* here refers to the action of the ointment. According to our understanding of the Chinese word for ointment, it can be a noun referring to the ointment itself or a verb referring to the action of the ointment. In Greek, this word is used not as a noun or as a verb but as a gerund; it does not refer to the ointment but to the function of the ointment. This is a function of grace, and this function is the anointing of grace. Thus it is not bad that the Chinese Union Version uses an expression here that means *unction of grace*. The New Testament Recovery Version in Chinese directly uses an expression which literally means *ointment-anointing*.

We must understand the thought of 1 John. First the blood cleanses us, then the ointment anoints us. It is as if we were treating a wound on our physical body; first we cleanse it, then we rub on some medicinal ointment. In the same way, the blood first cleanses us and then the ointment of God, which is the Spirit of God and God Himself, comes to anoint the place which has just been cleansed by the blood. In this way we obtain not only forgiveness through the blood but also God Himself by the anointing.

Now this ointment remains in us constantly, anointing us continuously. In other words, God Himself functions within us to anoint us with His substance. This is like painting; you apply and spread the substance of the paint onto a surface. In the same way, God operates and functions within us to anoint

His own substance and element into us. This causes us to subjectively know God Himself.

The Fellowship of the Divine Life

Most people know God as a God outside of them who is on high. This is an objective, outward knowing. Our God, however, is our Redeemer today, and by the cleansing of His blood and by His becoming the Spirit He now abides in us. He anoints us inwardly, painting His substance and element into us. Thus, we have a feeling within us and know that God wants to do a certain thing, so we follow Him to do it. At other times we know that God does not want to do a certain thing, so we do not do it.

This kind of knowing is not obtained from an outward, objective knowledge. Instead, it is received subjectively from the inward anointing. For example, small children like to eat sweet things and hate to eat bitter things. This knowledge does not require outward teaching. Rather, it is the knowing a child possesses naturally, and this knowledge comes from the nature of life. The life of the little child naturally wants sweet things and hates bitter things. This knowledge of sweet and bitter does not come from outward teachings but from an inward function of life. This function is a kind of knowledge that is subjective, not objective.

The anointing is God's functioning within us. He is our life. As the Spirit, He dispenses Himself into us as life. Thus, the anointing is the anointing of God, of the Holy Spirit—of the Spirit and of life. By this anointing of life, we can walk in fellowship with God. We must have this anointing before we can have fellowship with God and before we can live in this fellowship.

John's Gospel speaks of grace and truth, whereas John's Epistle unveils that the fellowship of the divine life brings us to the very sources of grace and truth, which are love and light. The truth is the shining and the expression of light. For example, if there were no shining of light here, this place would be dark, and we would not be able to see anyone's face; but once the light shines, everyone's real condition is manifested and everything becomes clear. In the same way, love is the source of grace, and grace is the manifestation of love. God Himself is love and also light. Therefore, if we remain in the anointing and walk in the fellowship of life, we enjoy God Himself, and the substance of God, which is love and light, is anointed into us. The expression of love is grace, and the manifestation of light is truth. Hallelujah, how good this is!

The anointing refers to a central matter, that we who believe into the Lord and are saved need to abide in the Lord to enjoy His life. The Lord has given us His life, and this life is simply Himself in us as life. We who are saved need to enjoy this life every day. In the preceding chapters we pointed out repeatedly the way to abide in the Lord in order to be able to enjoy Him as our life. In this chapter our subject is "Experiencing the Cleansing of the Lord's Blood and Enjoying the Anointing of the Holy Ointment." According to the truth of the Bible, this is a solid and profound matter.

EXPERIENCING THE CLEANSING
OF THE LORD'S BLOOD

Forgiveness and Cleansing

Experiencing the cleansing of the Lord's blood and enjoying the anointing of the holy ointment are completely different from most people's concept. The Lord's blood first cleanses us, then the holy ointment anoints us. This is explained very clearly in the first two chapters of 1 John and is something that is according to God's economy, but this matter does not exist in most people's concept. Many people feel that since they have offended man and God, they must beg God to forgive and pardon them. They may never think that the blood can cleanse people. In most people's concept, the sight of blood is frightening and any blood that is sprinkled onto people makes their body dirty, so they may wonder how the blood could cleanse them. We can see how the matter of forgiveness and cleansing goes against the average person's concept.

In God's concept, however, we are fallen, sinful people. Our sin does not merely need forgiveness; it also needs cleansing. For example, when you get your clothes dirty, it is an offense to your mother. Even though your mother forgives you, the dirt is still on your clothing and needs to be washed off. In the same way, to forgive, to pardon, is one thing, while to cleanse, to remove the stain of sin, is another. Therefore, 1 John 1:9 says that God not only forgives us but also cleanses us. Forgiving is to forgive the trespass, and cleansing is to wash away the stain of the trespass.

Before God and according to His law, we have sins and trespasses, while as to our person, our being, we have been stained. For our trespasses we need God's forgiveness; for our stains we need God's cleansing, which is by the precious blood. First John 2 says that after being cleansed, we have received something of grace from the Holy One. Within us there is something that is constantly moving and anointing, which is the holy ointment. Actually, this holy ointment is God Himself coming into us to anoint us based on the cleansing of the blood.

The Type in the Old Testament

Despite the fact that this matter is clearly explained in 1 John, it is still not easy for us to understand because the human concept does not have this thought and because it is very deep, mysterious, and abstract. In the Old Testament, however, this thought can be seen in the type of the cleansing of the leper. Leprosy does not begin from the outside but from within; then it appears outwardly to become an uncleanness. Leprosy signifies sin. Sin does not first harm our outward actions. Rather, it first enters our nature to corrupt it, and then it breaks forth from our nature and is manifested outwardly to also corrupt our outward actions.

A leper was condemned before God, and his person was unclean. Therefore, he needed God's forgiveness on the one hand and the cleansing of his being on the other hand. Leviticus 14 says that before he could be cleansed, he had to offer a trespass offering and a sin offering (vv. 12, 19). The trespass offering was for the outward deeds, the trespasses, and the sin offering was for the inward nature, the sin. Fallen man has contracted leprosy, having an inward sinful nature that is manifested as the outward sinful deeds. Moreover, he is unclean before God. Therefore, he must be forgiven before he can be cleansed. This is why he first needs to offer to God two kinds of offerings—the sin offering and the trespass offering. These two offerings typify the Lord Jesus as our Redeemer who accomplished redemption for us.

Leviticus 14 shows that when the one asking for cleansing had been forgiven through the offering of the sacrifices, the priest took the blood shed from these two sacrifices and put it on the person's ear, thumb, and toe (v. 14). The ear is for hearing, the hand is for doing, and the foot is for walking. Man commits sins because of these three members. For example, a young student first hears his classmates at school describing how they stole their fathers' money, and the sinful nature within him rises up in response. Then he walks home and uses his hands to do the same thing. Thus, he successfully commits a sin, and the leprosy has come out into the open. We thank the Lord that Christ died for us, for our sin, and for our sins, our trespasses. Now through the offering of the Lord Jesus as our sin offering and our trespass offering we are redeemed from sin. However, we are still not cleansed, so we must apply the redeeming blood on our ear, thumb, and toe to obtain cleansing.

After the cleansing, the priest brought the oil and sprinkled it seven times before God. Then he put it on the ear, thumb, and toe upon which the blood had been applied; that is, he put the oil upon the blood. Following this he poured the remainder of the oil on the person's head (vv. 15-18). In this way, the person became a son of oil (Zech. 4:14). Because he had been washed by the blood and then anointed with the oil, he was cleansed.

The natural man cannot understand this kind of truth and finds it very strange. Generally people think that Christianity instructs people how to worship God, fear God, and honor God. Then it teaches people to be faithful, righteous, and peaceable. It also teaches people to have filial respect, brotherly affection, and benevolence. It is true that the Bible does mention these things and even says much about them; nevertheless, the basic concept of the Bible is focused on the blood and the oil. God wants to sprinkle us sinners with the

blood; then He wants to anoint us with oil. Wherever the
blood is sprinkled, there the oil is applied. In this way we
have become those who are sprinkled by the blood. Furthermore, we have become those who have the anointing; that is,
we have become sons of oil. Thus, we are cleansed and can
enter into the fellowship of the eternal life.

THE FELLOWSHIP OF THE ETERNAL LIFE

Hence, in the New Testament, the apostle John first wrote
his Gospel telling us that Jesus Christ was God who came in
the flesh and died for us; then in resurrection He became the
life-giving Spirit to give us the eternal life. When we believe
and receive Him, He comes into us as the life-giving Spirit
and gives us the eternal life. Thus, we are regenerated to
become the children of God. Then John continued his writings
with 1 John, telling us that whoever is regenerated with the
life of God to be a child of God has this eternal life inside him
and that this life brings a fellowship.

Most people do not adequately understand the meaning of
fellowship; the average Christian may even think that it
means "social contact." The Bible, however, does not say *social
contact* but *fellowship.* In Greek, this word *fellowship* is
koinonia, which refers to several people or objects that can
be mixed together and mingled thoroughly. For example,
lightbulbs are mingled into one flow, because within them
they all have the current of electricity from the electric plant
and are all blended in one flow; hence, they have "fellowship"
with one another. Therefore, we may explain fellowship as a
flow, but we cannot say that it is a social contact.

The best illustration of fellowship is the circulation of
blood in the body. The blood in the human body circulates very
quickly; before we have finished speaking one sentence, the
blood has already been circulating. That circulation is a
fellowship to the body. The circulation of blood is a flow, but to
all the members of the body it is a fellowship. Because of this
fellowship our ears and our feet are connected even though
they do not grow next to one another. When I am speaking
here, my mouth is not the only part working, all of my members are cooperating. Even my hair is moving, and this is all

because of the circulation of the blood that joins all the members in one fellowship and makes them one.

REMAINING IN THE FELLOWSHIP OF THE DIVINE LIFE BY CONFESSING TO GOD

The divine life, like the current of electricity and the circulation of blood, is always flowing. First John 1:7 says, "If we walk in the light as He is in the light, we have fellowship with one another, and the blood of Jesus His Son cleanses us from every sin." This means that when we believed in the Lord Jesus, the eternal life entered into us and brought with it the fellowship of life. Therefore, we must remain in this fellowship, and then the Lord's blood will cleanse us from our sins. Regrettably, this fellowship within many saved ones has stopped and is interrupted. With regard to the spiritual life, these people are deadened.

Furthermore, although we have believed in the Lord Jesus, our sins have been forgiven, and we have been saved, our inward nature still exists and the root of our sinning is still there. In the last century, there were some in Christianity who said that once a person is regenerated, sin is eradicated from him. This kind of teaching still exists today. However, John says that we who are saved and regenerated and even have God's life within us do not have sin eradicated from our being. He says, "If we say that we do not have sin, we are deceiving ourselves" (1 John 1:8). In Greek, the word for *sin* here is singular, referring to the sinful nature. This sinful nature is the root of the sinful deeds (v. 7) we commit.

Because man has a sinning life, he commits sins. The older a person becomes, the more abundant his fruits of sin are. Before God every person has sinned; there are no exceptions. Of all the people born on earth, there is none who does not steal or lie. It is natural for people to lie; it is unusual when they do not lie. The so-called tactful people are just good liars. Courtesy is often a game of playing politics. If someone would say that he has never stolen anything or that he has never lied, he is the top sinner because he has not told the truth. We believers in Christ do not like to scold others. Rather, we like to speak the truth in love, and what we actually want to do is to preach the gospel and proclaim the truth. All the people in the world are cheating one another; only the Lord's life is truth.

With the exception of the Lord Jesus, we do not believe that there is any perfect, holy person. Only the Lord Jesus is absolutely without sin. As those who have been saved by grace, we have the Lord's life and His Holy Spirit. We need to pray unceasingly, to be in fear and trembling, and to exercise to walk according to the Spirit. However, whenever we are a little careless or loose, our flesh immediately comes out. I can testify that even though I do not commit big sins every day, at the end of each day before I go to sleep, I still need to confess and repent. Although I did not steal anything or tell any lies, I am not happy within. Of course, this unhappiness is not from the Lord but from myself and my flesh.

For the sake of my health, my wife does not allow me to eat carelessly. Sometimes people give me things to eat, but she hides them from me; then when the grandchildren come, she brings them out. When I find out about this, my heart is not happy. Of course, it is not the Lord Jesus who is unhappy within me; rather, it is I who am unhappy. Although I have not committed a gross sin such as fighting with my wife, I have committed the cultured, refined sin of being secretly angry and unhappy within. Therefore, every evening as I consider, I always discover that I did a number of things not in my spirit and without living Christ; I was altogether in myself. I confess all these things one by one.

I believe that many brothers and sisters love the Lord and have been in the church life for many years, yet they have the same "sickness" and are in the same condition that I am in. This is our problem. Even though the brothers know that they should live Christ and walk according to the Spirit, they get angry inwardly when their wives hide things from them. The sisters all say that they want to live Christ and walk in the Spirit, but whenever they pick up the telephone and begin talking, they cannot put it down. These matters all indicate that we truly need the Lord's salvation.

Perhaps we have been saved for many years. We love the Lord, are experienced in spiritual matters, and have some experience in life, but as soon as we leave the fellowship of the divine life, we have no way to walk in the light. We may use a lightbulb to illustrate this. It does not matter how long a lightbulb has been shining or how experienced it is; as soon as the electrical current is cut off, it cannot shine. Our breathing is another illustration. No one can say that because he has breathed for many years and is very experienced, he can stop breathing for a few days. It does not matter how much experience you have in breathing; as soon as you stop breathing, you will immediately die. In the same way, we cannot depend on our years of experience in the matter of the fellowship of the divine life. We must continue non-stop in this fellowship.

We all must see that even though we have been saved, we must humble ourselves. We still have the sinful nature, and we still commit sins. Perhaps we do not commit big sins or gross sins, but we constantly commit small sins. Sometimes we get upset just because of what other people say, and we become unhappy within. All people are the descendants of fallen Adam. Even if we are moral and righteous, no one is without sin or offense before God. Our nature is just sin. Therefore, we must confess our sins daily before the Lord. We have discovered all this from our actual experience.

By way of illustration, an apple tree is not an apple tree because it bears apples; rather, it bears apples because it is an apple tree. Even if, for some reason, it does not bear apples for many years, it is still an apple tree. In the same way, you may be very moral and righteous today because you are in a good environment which does not give you the opportunity to commit sins. If your environment were to change, however, you may not be so good. Moreover, we have the sinful nature within us and are sinners by birth. Hence, whether or not we sin in deeds, still we all are sinners.

This is why we deceive ourselves if we say that we do not have sin. If we say that we do not have sin, we consider God a liar, because the Bible clearly says, "All have sinned and fall short of the glory of God....Through one man sin entered into the world, and through sin, death; and thus death passed on to all men because all have sinned" (Rom. 3:23; 5:12). The fact that all men die proves that all have sinned. How can a person say that he does not have sin? If he really had no sin, then God could be considered a liar because He said that all have sinned.

GOD FORGIVING OUR SINS

God cannot lie. If we speak the truth, we must confess that we have a sinful nature within and sinful deeds without. Hence, we are bona fide sinners. Perhaps in the eyes of men, you are a perfect gentleman, one who is filled with a sense of justice. Before God, however, you cannot say that you have no sins or trespasses outwardly, nor can you deny that you have a sinful nature inwardly. Thus, we all need God's forgiveness. But how does God forgive us? He does not sit on high in the heavens with majesty and authority, saying, "Because I love you, I erase your debt of sin and forgive you." If He did it in this way, He would be a loose, careless, unrighteous God. The Bible reveals that God is a God of principle, a God who is righteous and holy; He cannot do things in a way that would violate His holy nature or His righteous character. He must do things that are judicially righteous.

The Bible indicates that the first step God took in saving us sinners was to be incarnated as a man, and this man was called Jesus Christ. Jesus Christ was God incarnated, a true man with a body of bones, blood, and flesh; He was a man with real human blood. Therefore, He was qualified to be the Substitute for humanity in shedding His blood and dying for man. Furthermore, the Lord Jesus did not become a full-grown man in the twinkling of an eye. He was not born one day, crucified the next, and raised and raptured on the following day. He was incarnated according to the laws of creation by being conceived in the womb of a virgin. He remained there for nine months and then was born as a baby. He then lived the human life on earth according to the laws of human growth.

It seems the Lord Jesus did not do anything in His first thirty years except to live as a true man in the home of Joseph, a carpenter, whom others thought was His father. He truly and actually passed through the trials and tribulations of human life. When He was thirty years old, He came out to minister, preaching the truth, healing the sick, casting out demons, and releasing the people who were oppressed by sin. After ministering for three and a half years, He personally delivered Himself up to the cross as the Substitute for all men, using His real human body with its human life and nature to vicariously take God's punishment on the cross for us, shedding His real human blood to cleanse us from our sins. In this way He accomplished the work of redeeming us so that God could legally forgive us. This was truly a marvelous work!

THE ALL-INCLUSIVE HOLY ANOINTING OINTMENT

In the universe there are two great, marvelous matters: one is God's incarnation and the other is His death on the cross with His resurrection in which He became the life-giving Spirit. In His incarnation the Lord became a man of flesh and blood with God in Him, and as the last Adam who passed through death and resurrection, He became the life-giving Spirit. Today this life-giving Spirit is both God and man, both the Creator and the Redeemer, even the Savior. As the Redeemer He died on the cross for us to redeem us from the curse of sin, and as the Savior He enters into us to save us from the bondage of sin, the world, and the flesh. Moreover, as the life-giving Spirit, He enters into us not merely to give us life but also to be our life.

This Spirit is the all-inclusive Spirit, who comprises God, man, the Redeemer, the Savior, the life-giving Lord, and the Holy Spirit. This Spirit also includes all the experiences of the trials, tribulations, and bitterness which the Lord passed through in His human life on earth. Moreover, this Spirit includes the Lord's death and resurrection on the third day with their efficacy. So now the Spirit is an extraordinary Spirit, a mingled and all-inclusive Spirit.

In Exodus 30 there is a type of the Spirit—the holy anointing ointment. The holy anointing ointment is made of one hin of olive oil (signifying the unique God) with four ancient spices (signifying the four living creatures, the creation): myrrh and cassia, five hundred shekels each; and cinnamon and calamus, two hundred fifty shekels each. The four kinds of spices are of three units with the middle unit split into two, signifying that the middle One of the Divine Trinity was split and died for us on the cross, and in resurrection He was completely mingled with us. This is the holy anointing ointment typifying the all-inclusive life-giving Spirit.

In this Spirit, who is typified by the ointment, there are God, man, the experience of human life with its trials and tribulations, the death on the cross, the power of death, resurrection, the power of resurrection, and all that He is, such as His human virtues and divine attributes. All these items were compounded into the Spirit. Therefore, this Spirit is the Triune God, our Lord Jesus, the Creator, the Redeemer, the Savior, the life-giving Spirit, and life, compounded with all the items of His human living, His death, His resurrection, and all that He is. Moreover, Revelation tells us that this Spirit has been intensified sevenfold. What a Spirit!

Today, all that the Lord Jesus is and all that He has accomplished are written in great detail in the Bible. This Bible is the gospel; the content of the gospel we preach today is the entire Bible. We thank and praise Him that as the Spirit He is experientially real. When we preach the Bible, this Spirit comes along. The same is true when we read the Bible because this Spirit, who is God and the Lord Jesus, cannot be separated from the word of the Bible.

When you hear the gospel, when you hear people preaching the Bible, your spirit within you is moved because your spirit can touch this Spirit, who is God Himself, that is, the Lord Jesus Himself. When He moves you and your heart turns to Him, you feel that you need Jesus, that your life is vain, and that you are a sinner without hope in the world. You feel that you have been struggling and laboring, and that even if you have some fame or accomplishment, it has no meaning. What is there in the end? What will the future be? Your heart turns and you call, "O Lord, I have sinned! O Lord, I need You!" As soon as you call, you have believed and you are saved. Many believers prayed very simple prayers when they were saved. Nevertheless, their heart turned and their mouth called. As soon as they opened their mouth to pray, the Spirit entered into them and they were saved.

THE SIGNIFICANCE OF THE PRECIOUS BLOOD
AND THE HOLY OINTMENT

What is the precious blood? It is the Lord's blood. The Lord's blood indicates the redemption accomplished by the Lord. Through His incarnation, human living, death, and resurrection He accomplished the work of redemption. In the Bible, the work which the Lord accomplished by His being processed is called redemption, and it is symbolized by the blood. Thus, the blood represents redemption, which includes the Lord's incarnation, human living, death, and resurrection. What then is the ointment? We have already seen that the ointment is God Himself who is the Spirit. Our God became flesh as the Lord Jesus; He passed through human living, death, and resurrection, thereby accomplishing redemption. Then in resurrection, He became the life-giving Spirit. The Spirit includes all that Christ is. Thus, the blood, representing His redemption, refers to what He has accomplished, while the Spirit, representing all that He is, refers to what He is.

Your being sprinkled by the blood indicates that you have been redeemed. All the negative things and the problems of sin can never bother you again. Because of the blood, God forgives all your sins and erases all your offenses. After the sprinkling of the blood, the Spirit as the ointment—what God is—follows to anoint you inwardly. God is life; He is also love, light, holiness, righteousness, and power. This anointing anoints all that God is into you, giving you all of God's being. The Lord's blood cleanses us, and the ointment anoints us. In this way the redemption God accomplished and all the riches of His being are fully applied to us through our believing.

I am very happy today because I am a person who has been cleansed by the blood and who has obtained God Himself. I was a sinner, a fallen and corrupted person, but my God, who accomplished redemption for me, sprinkled the blood upon me, a symbol of His redemption, and cleansed my entire being for me to receive His redemption and all that He has accomplished. At the same time He also anointed into me what He is, His very being, represented by the ointment. Thus, even today, we who believe in the Lord have the precious blood and the holy ointment. Hallelujah, how wonderful this is!

ABIDING IN THE LORD AND ENJOYING HIS LIFE
THROUGH THE BLOOD AND THE OINTMENT

As soon as we are saved, we obtain the fellowship of the divine life. However, the inward sinful nature and the outward sinful acts always become a problem to us, as we have described above. Both gross sins and trivial sins block our fellowship with God and give us a sense of guilt. Therefore, if we want to remain in the fellowship of the divine life, the first thing we must do is confess our sins to God. First John 1:7-9 says that whenever we are in the light, we confess our sins. When we are not in the light, we do not feel that we have sin; once we are in the light, however, we feel that we truly have sinned. As soon as we confess our sins, the Lord forgives us. If we are in darkness though, we will only see the sins of others without seeing our own sins. In that condition we cannot confess our sins, and the Lord's blood cannot cleanse us from our sins.

In other words, whenever we come to God and feel that we are wrong or we have a guilty feeling, that means we are in the light. Spontaneously, we ask the Lord to forgive us of our sins. Once we confess our sins, God is faithful to forgive us of our sins. He is also righteous, so He must cleanse us from all our sins through the blood of Jesus. The cleansing of the precious blood brings in the anointing of the holy ointment. This anointing teaches us how to live and walk.

Thus, the next time you are about to get angry, the anointing will immediately remind you that you must walk by the anointing. You can be angry only when the anointing is angry; when the anointing is not angry, you cannot be angry. When the anointing says, "Hallelujah," you must also say, "Hallelujah." All our deeds and actions must follow the teaching of the anointing. In this way our entire living will be one of experiencing the cleansing of the precious blood and enjoying the anointing of the holy ointment. Then we will abide in the Lord and enjoy His life.

A life of abiding in the Lord and enjoying His life is a life in which we constantly experience the cleansing of the blood and enjoy the anointing moment by moment. Whenever you have even a slight feeling that something is wrong or have the sense that you are living in the flesh, in the old creation, or in the self, you should immediately confess your sin and ask for the Lord's forgiveness. When you confess according to this sense, it proves that you are in the light. Then the blood cleanses you, and the anointing follows to anoint you, increasing the element of God within you. You then enjoy more of what God is. You are practically abiding in the Lord and enjoying His life.

ABOUT THE AUTHOR

Witness Lee was born in 1905 in northern China and raised in a Christian family. At age 19 he was fully captured for Christ and immediately consecrated himself to preach the gospel for the rest of his life. Early in his service, he met Watchman Nee, a renowned preacher, teacher, and writer. Witness Lee labored together with Watchman Nee under his direction. In 1934 Watchman Nee entrusted Witness Lee with the responsibility for his publication operation, called the Shanghai Gospel Bookroom.

Prior to the Communist takeover in 1949, Witness Lee was sent by Watchman Nee and his other co-workers to Taiwan to ensure that the things delivered to them by the Lord would not be lost. Watchman Nee instructed Witness Lee to continue the former's publishing operation abroad as the Taiwan Gospel Bookroom, which has been publicly recognized as the publisher of Watchman Nee's works outside China. Witness Lee's work in Taiwan manifested the Lord's abundant blessing. From a mere 350 believers, newly fled from the mainland, the churches in Taiwan grew to 20,000 in five years.

In 1962 Witness Lee felt led of the Lord to come to the United States, settling in California. During his 35 years of service in the U.S., he ministered in weekly meetings and weekend conferences, delivering several thousand spoken messages. Much of his speaking has since been published as over 400 titles. Many of these have been translated into over fourteen languages. He gave his last public conference in February 1997 at the age of 91.

He leaves behind a prolific presentation of the truth in the Bible. His major work, *Life-study of the Bible,* comprises over 25,000 pages of commentary on every book of the Bible from the perspective of the believers' enjoyment and experience of God's divine life in Christ through the Holy Spirit. Witness Lee was the chief editor of a new translation of the New Testament into Chinese called the Recovery Version and directed the translation of the same into English. The Recovery Version also appears in a number of other languages. He provided an extensive body of footnotes, outlines, and spiritual cross references. A radio broadcast of his messages can be heard on Christian radio stations in the United States. In 1965 Witness Lee founded Living Stream Ministry, a non-profit corporation, located in Anaheim, California, which officially presents his and Watchman Nee's ministry.

Witness Lee's ministry emphasizes the experience of Christ as life and the practical oneness of the believers as the Body of Christ. Stressing the importance of attending to both these matters, he led the churches under his care to grow in Christian life and function. He was unbending in his conviction that God's goal is not narrow sectarianism but the Body of Christ. In time, believers began to meet simply as the church in their localities in response to this conviction. In recent years a number of new churches have been raised up in Russia and in many eastern European countries.